No Excuses

Lessons from
21 High-Performing, High-Poverty Schools

Samuel Casey Carter

Foreword by
Adam Meyerson

The Heritage Foundation
214 Massachusetts Avenue, NE
Washington, DC 20002
202-546-4400
www.heritage.org

Cover photo courtesy of Cornerstone Schools Association
Photo illustration by Mitzi Hamilton
Cover design by Michelle F. Smith

ISBN 0-89195-090-7

Dedication

This book is dedicated to Suzanne Kirby, my wife,
and Kirby Catherine, our daughter.

No Excuses Campaign

The No Excuses campaign is a national effort organized by The Heritage Foundation to mobilize public pressure on behalf of better education for the poor. The No Excuses campaign brings together liberals, centrists, and conservatives who are committed to high academic achievement among children of all races, ethnic groups, and family incomes.

Participants in the No Excuses campaign may hold differing views about vouchers, the federal role in education, and other policy issues. But we agree that there is no excuse for the academic failure of most public schools serving poor children. All children can learn. Hundreds of public, private, and religious schools serving low-income children have proved it. Help us to shine a spotlight on their success and join us in demanding that failing schools meet their standard.

No Excuses.

Table of Contents

Acknowledgments

The original idea for this project was first conceived by Adam Meyerson. Without his regular guidance, the final product would be half what it is today. In addition, he supported this research with the full resources of The Heritage Foundation's Civil Society Project. In particular, Mary Siddall, Shawnna Matthews, and Hunter Campaigne are responsible for making the No Excuses Campaign a reality. Jill Abraham, Hans Allhoff, and John DeGroot provided me invaluable help as research assistants. Their work runs throughout these pages.

Several other people—whether through sustained help or a single phone call—contributed enormously to my understanding of the subject and pointed me in the right direction: Jeanne Allen, Ray Anderson, Tracey Bailey, Merrill Bargo, Stephanie Bell-Rose, Muriel Berkeley, Sue Bodilly, Peggy Brown, Doug Carnine, Maria Casilas, Linda Clarke, Wayne Comora, Wade Curry, Murray Dickman, Dick Elmer, Robert C. Embry, Jr., Checker Finn, Steven Fleischman, Howard Fuller, David Garcia, Tom Glennan, Garry Huggins, Joe Johnson, Richard Kohr, Howard Lappin, Gail Levin, Patti Likens, Kevin MacGulicutty, Bruno Manno, Mike McKeown, Hans Meeder, L. Scott Miller, Anita Nestor, Abner Oakes, Mike Petrilli, Chuck Pizer, Ben Rarick, Robb Rauh, Nina Shokraii Rees, Douglas Reeves, Lucille Remnick, Jerry Richardson, Ken Rolling, Jerry Silbert, Laurie Slobody, Tim Slocum, Teresa Staten, Jennifer Stevens, Sam Stringfield, Ron Tamas, Abigail Thernstrom, Victoria Thorp, Mark Vignati, Mike Watson, Maurice Weavers, William Weichun, Amy Wilkins, Darv Winick, Kenneth K. Wong, and Cheri Yecke.

Special thanks must also go to the Lynde and Harry Bradley Foundation, which supports the Bradley Fellows program at The Heritage Foundation.

Foreword

A tenured teacher recently came to my office and told me, "These children can't learn. It's cultural." So, I looked at the lady, and I said, "You're coming from 72nd Street, all the way up to Harlem, to tell me that children of color cannot learn?" I said to her, "You've got two choices. Either resign or I'm going to fire you." And you know what, she left, quickly. Because I made her life miserable. I observed her every single day, and I told her she couldn't teach, and she had to go. And she left. Good principals know the union contract. Good principals weed out ineffective teachers.

—Gregory Hodge, principal
Frederick Douglass Academy, Harlem

Aristotle said that we can demonstrate the possible by studying the actual. This remarkable book by Samuel Casey Carter shows what is possible in the education of low-income children.

The failure of most public schools to teach poor children is a national tragedy and a national disgrace. Fifty-eight percent of low-income 4th graders cannot read, and 61 percent of low-income 8th graders cannot do basic math. The magnitude of this educational malpractice is staggering: Of the roughly 20 million low-income children in K–12 schools, 12 million aren't even learning the most elementary skills. These children have little hope of mastering the responsibilities of citizenship or the rigors of global competition.

The message of this book is that there is no excuse for this tragedy. All children can learn. The principals and schools profiled in this book have overcome the bureaucratic and cultural obstacles that keep low-income children behind in most public schools. No Excuses schools have created a culture of achievement among children whom most public schools would condemn to a life of failure.

Success stories such as these have been told before. The great economist Thomas Sowell was writing about high-performing inner-city schools more than twenty years ago. William Bennett publicized such schools when he was Secretary of Education under President Reagan, and Richard Riley, who occupies the same post under President Clinton, has done the same. The legendary math teacher Jaime Escalante, who turned Garfield High School in the barrios of East Los Angeles into one of the top-ten AP calculus programs in the country, even inspired a Hollywood movie, *Stand and Deliver*.

But the reaction of the education establishment and its apologists has been to dismiss such achievement as a fluke—the work of extraordinary heroes whose performance cannot possibly be held as a national standard. As the *New York Times Magazine* put it in a recent cover story, entitled "What No School Can Do": "A child living in an inner city is in school for only so many hours. It's the rest of the day—as well as the rest of the neighborhood—that's the big influence, and the big problem."

Casey Carter's book drives a stake through this culture of defeatism. Educational excellence among low-income children can no longer be seen as the work of isolated superstars. Casey Carter found not one or two high-performing, high-poverty schools. He found twenty-one high-performing, high-poverty schools that put the public school establishment to shame. Their achievement is not an accident. Their success is the intended result of hard work, common sense teaching philosophies, and successful leadership strategies that can be replicated. One of the nation's highest priorities should be to learn from the best practices of these high-performing schools and to insist that all schools serving low-income children aspire to the No Excuses standard of excellence.

This study is not anti-public-school. It is, however, a damning indictment of public education as currently structured. Most of the high-achievement schools profiled in this book are *public schools*. But they have succeeded in spite of, not because of, the incentive structure and the culture of public education today. That incentive structure has to be completely overhauled, and the culture of excuses replaced by a culture of achievement, if No Excuses schools are to become the rule rather than the exception.

This book does not lay out a public policy blueprint for reforming education of the poor. However, the achievements of the No Excuses principals do have a number of important policy implications that deserve to be explored more fully in later studies.

Children of all races and income levels can meet high academic standards.

The schools profiled in this book hold all students, of all races and income levels, to high standards and expectations—and then make sure that all children succeed.

No Excuses principals reject the ideology of victimhood that dominates most public discussion of race and academic achievement. They do not dumb down tests and courses for black and Hispanic children; instead they prove that children of all races and income levels can take tough courses and succeed. They recognize that some children may learn at different paces, but they make sure that all children master key subjects, especially reading, math, and fluency in the English language. They test constantly, for tests are the best way to determine whether each and every child is learning: the No Excuses principals see testing as an instrument of diagnosis, not of discrimination. Nor do they think that social promotion is any favor to children; they do not hesitate to require students to repeat grades, if necessary to master the material.

No Excuses principals hold teachers to the same high standards they hold students. Teachers who cannot achieve high performance among low-income students, even after training from master teachers, must look quickly for another job.

Running a high-poverty school is one of the most important leadership positions in America.

No single curriculum or teaching methodology is the secret to the success of the high-performing schools in this study. What they all have in common is excellent *leadership*. Almost every one of the No Excuses schools in this book created a culture of outstanding academic achievement within four to five years. Some were new schools that started from scratch. In most cases, they were low-performing schools that became high performers once the right leadership took over.

The high-performing principals in this study have a number of distinctive competencies. Many are superb at working with parents and enlisting their active support for the school's mission. Many are skilled administrators and problem-solvers who stretch the dollars in their meager budgets and create happy, orderly environments in old worn-down buildings. But above all what distinguishes the No Excuses principals is their skill in finding, training, and bringing out the best in teachers. No Excuses schools are schools where good teachers thrive and develop into great teachers.

This suggests that the recruitment of excellent principals for high-poverty schools is one of the best ways to expand opportunity for low-income children. Finding the right principals, who in turn will find the right teachers, may be more important than reducing class size, modernizing school facilities, or any of the conventional nostrums for improving public education.

To attract and keep great leaders may require paying them as great leaders. Principals who perform well, close to the standard set by No Excuses schools, should be generously rewarded. Large urban school systems could easily find funds for this purpose by reducing the size of their central administrations. Private philanthropists could also step in to reward and encourage exceptional leadership.

Most principals of high-poverty schools do not come close to the standard set by No Excuses principals. They should be replaced.

High achievement requires freedom.

The high-performing principals in this study have enjoyed unusual freedom to make important decisions for their schools. They have hired and fired teachers. They have set their own budgets. In some cases they have chosen the curriculum. The charter-school principals in this study have been given this freedom explicitly in their charters. Private-school principals also have substantial decision-making power, subject to approval by their boards of trustees.

The public-school principals in this study have taken this freedom: They have found a way to free themselves from many of the personnel regulations, line-by-line budget requirements, and curricular mandates that hamstring most public-school principals.

If we want to attract exceptional leaders to high-poverty schools, we have to free principals from micromanagement, and give them the freedom No Excuses principals have enjoyed. Principals can excel if they are given the opportunity to do their jobs as they see fit—while being held strictly accountable for academic achievement. There will be no excuse for student failure if principals are given both the freedom and the responsibility to make their schools successful.

Education schools and teacher certification requirements need a complete overhaul.

Teacher training is central to the effectiveness of the schools in this study. But most No Excuses principals say that current certification requirements bear little relation to quality teaching, and that education schools are woefully inadequate in training teachers for low-income children.

The principals in this study sharply criticize the teaching philosophies that have dominated education schools for the past generation. They reject whole language, whole math, developmentally-appropriate education, and other teaching theories that deemphasize the acquisition of skills. They teach science, music, and history, not self-esteem. They say the best head start any poor child can have is rigorous instruction in reading and math, beginning in kindergarten.

The principals in this study also fault education schools for failing to study and learn from success. No Excuses schools have a superb track record of training teachers on site. But most of the high-performing, high-poverty schools profiled in this book have never been studied by leading education journals or teachers' colleges. Business schools study successful business practice. Medical schools study successful medical practice. It's time for education schools to study systematically the principals and teachers who know how to improve the academic performance of their students, regardless of their race or family background.

Parents eagerly send their children to high-performance schools.

This study of high-performing principals does not speak directly to the desirability of school vouchers, tuition tax credits, or other proposals to increase parental choice and competition. The principals themselves come out on both sides of this issue.

However, the experience of No Excuses principals shows that high-performing schools would have nothing to fear and everything to gain from reform proposals that give parents more say about where to send their children. Parents are already clamoring to send their children to No Excuses schools. A number of schools in this study were neighborhood public schools that were about to be closed because of insufficient enrollment; enrollment rose rapidly as soon as achievement soared. Long waiting lists have developed at the charter schools in this study, as well as the public schools where students can transfer within or across district lines.

High achievement is also the recipe for voluntary racial and economic integration. White parents began sending their children to Portland Elementary in rural Arkansas as test scores of black students there rose dramatically. Middle-class parents started transferring their children to Morse Elementary in Cambridge, Massachusetts, as test scores of low-income children rose rapidly.

To increase choice for parents, especially in low-income neighbor-hoods, will require more than opening up access to private schools. It also requires freeing up inner-city public schools so that they can com-pete effectively for parents' support. No Excuses schools already enjoy the freedom to be excellent, and they have won the enthusiastic com-mitment of parents who want their children to succeed. Isn't it time for the public education establishment to allow all parents the opportunity for their children to achieve?

Adam Meyerson
Vice President, Educational Affairs
The Heritage Foundation

Introduction

America's public schools have utterly failed the poor. Over half of low-income 4th graders cannot read with understanding.[1] Almost two-thirds of low-income 8th graders cannot multiply or divide two-digit numbers.[2] At this rate, one out of four children in America go through school with no hope for the future. Apologists claim that the legacies of poverty, racism, and broken families cannot be overcome when it comes to educating our nation's neediest. They are wrong.

This book documents the success of twenty-one schools that refuse to make poverty an excuse for academic failure. These No Excuses schools are familiar with the challenges of educating the poor—three-quarters or more of their students qualify for the federal lunch program. Nonetheless, the schools studied here have building-wide median test scores above the 65th percentile on national academic achievement tests. Eleven of them score at or above the 80th percentile. By contrast, schools with similar numbers of poor children typically score below the 35th percentile.

Against the perennial claims of the education establishment that poor children are uneducable, these case studies highlight and celebrate the effective practices of low-income schools that work. Only by encourag-

Notes:

1. Patricia L. Donahue, *et al.*, *NAEP 1998 Reading Report Card for the Nation and the States*, National Center for Educational Statistics (March 1999), p. 81. This statistic represents the percentage of low-income 4th graders who scored below "basic" on the 1998 NAEP reading test. Low-income children are those who qualify for the free or reduced-price lunch in the federal school lunch program.
2. "By the Numbers: The Urban Picture—Poverty and Achievement in Urban and Nonurban Districts," *Education Week*, January 8, 1998, pp. 58-59. This statistic represents the percentage of low-income 8th graders who scored below "basic" on the 1996 NAEP math test.

ing, rewarding, and imitating this kind of success will our schools provide the kind of opportunity that all children in a free society deserve.

The schools highlighted here are a disparate but representative group. Three are charter schools. Three are private. One is religious. One is rural. Fifteen are public schools that draw the majority of their students from their local attendance zones—even if they hardly *act* like local public schools. They are just a sampling, but all in all, the stories told here represent the American experience of education north, south, east, and west—from the Bronx and Los Angeles to rural Arkansas.

For all their differences, these schools share certain traits and beliefs. Most notably, they all are led by strong principals who hold their students and their teachers to the highest standards. Every single one of them believes that children of all races and income levels can meet high academic standards.

Some people maintain that these schools are statistical anomalies, or "outliers" as the social scientists call them. The layman would say that these school principals are heroes—charismatic leaders—whose achievement, while inspirational, is not instructive for improving the school system as a whole.

The No Excuses principals are committed, innovative, and entrepreneurial individuals. Their efforts are extraordinary, often going beyond the call of duty. They and the schools they lead are exceptional and unique, it is true.

Yet, nothing these men and women do is beyond the reach of any school in the country. By studying the traits that these high-performing, high-poverty schools share, other schools can replicate their successes. They, too, can emulate the commitment, innovation, and entrepreneurial spirit that drive this kind of success and inspire this level of achievement in others.

Seven Common Traits of High-Performing, High-Poverty Schools

1. Principals must be free.

Effective principals decide how to spend their money, whom to hire, and what to teach. Unless principals are free to establish their own curricula, seek out their own faculties, and teach as they see fit, their teaching will not be its best.

Without freedom, a school principal is powerless. Effective principals either are given their freedom or take it for themselves. Principals whose schools develop a reputation for academic achievement usually are left alone; but in order to get there, great principals often are mavericks who buck the system or low flyers who get the job done quietly.

Schools serving low-income children are often poorly funded. Even on shoestring budgets, effective principals make their schools work, but innovation and flexibility are the keys to their success. Unless principals are free to spend their budgets as they see fit, their schools will be compromised.

2. Principals use measurable goals to establish a culture of achievement.

High expectations are one thing—the relentless pursuit of excellence is another. Tangible and unyielding goals are the focus of high-performing schools. Whether the goal is calculus by 12th grade, a fluently bilingual school, proficient musical performance for all, literacy at the earliest age, 100 percent attendance, or 100 percent working above grade level, great schools set hard and fast goals that the whole school must strive to obtain.

High expectations mean nothing if they are compromised in the classroom. Once the principal sets a clear vision for the school, *every* teacher has to be held *personally* responsible for enforcing it.

Outstanding middle schools and high schools focus on college preparation. In order to make achievement the product, great schools make college the goal.

3. Master teachers bring out the best in a faculty.

Improving the quality of instruction is the only way to improve overall student achievement. Teacher quality is the single most accurate indicator of a student's performance in school.[3]

Master teachers are the key to improved teacher quality. Master teachers often head peer evaluations, lead team teaching, devise internal assessment measures, and keep the mission of the school focused on academic achievement. Quality, not seniority, is the key.

Effective principals turn their schools into schools for teachers. They scour the country for the best teachers they can find and design their curriculum around the unique strengths and expertise of their staff. Master teachers help the faculty implement that curriculum.

Notes:

3. William L. Sanders and June C. Rivers, *Cumulative and Residual Effects of Teachers on Future Student Academic Achievement*, University of Tennessee Value-Added Research and Assessment Center, 1996, p. 6.

4. Rigorous and regular testing leads to continuous student achievement.

Modern-day reform jargon speaks of assessment and accountability. Principals of high-performing schools speak of testing.

High expectations without a means of measurement are hollow. Testing is the diagnostic tool that best enforces a school's goals. Regular testing at all levels and in all areas ensures that teaching and learning of the prescribed curriculum are taking place in every classroom. Mock tests usually are administered three or four times a year in preparation for the national exams.

Principals eliminate all excuses for failure by taking personal responsibility for the success of their children. As head of the instructional program, the principal does this best by *personally* monitoring the regular assessment of every child in the school. Teachers quickly learn that they too are tested each time they test their students.

5. Achievement is the key to discipline.

A command-and-control approach to discipline is limited by the number of guards you can hire. When self-discipline and order come from within, every extra person is part of the solution.

When a school clearly teaches by example that self-control, self-reliance, and self-esteem anchored in achievement are the means to success, that school's own success inspires confidence, order, and discipline in its students.

Effective principals hope to create lasting opportunities with life-long rewards for their students. Without apology, they allow the rigorous demands of achievement to show the way. Children need clear and conspicuous reasons to flee from error and run toward success. The demands of achievement provide both.

6. Principals work actively with parents to make the home a center of learning.

In high-poverty schools, a lack of parental involvement is often the first excuse for poor performance. Effective principals overcome this excuse by extending the mission of the school into the home.

Principals of high-performing schools *establish contracts* with parents to support their children's efforts to learn. In order to harness the benefits of parental support and motivation, effective principals teach parents to read to their children, check their homework, and ask after their assignments. In the end, however, *each student*, not a child's parents, is held accountable for his or her own success.

More than almost anything else, an outstanding school is a source of pride, a wellspring of joy, and a force for stability in an impoverished community. Great principals work with parents to make this happen.

7. Effort creates ability.

Time on task is the key to success in school. School is hard work, and great principals demand that their students work hard. Extended days, extended years, after-school programs, weekend programs, and summer school are all features of outstanding schools. None wastes time.

Effective principals eliminate social promotion. Students must fulfill very specific course requirements in order to advance either in class or on to the next grade level. No student is advanced without a clear demonstration of mastery.

Effective principals reject the notion that teaching is an 8 A.M. to 3 P.M. job. They expect the same of their teachers.

Effective Practices

The seven traits that all high-performing, high-poverty schools have in common give rise to a number of common practices. Although each school solves its own problems in its own way, a certain number of "best practices" emerge, and deserve study.

In particular, the effective practices of high-performing, high-poverty schools point out what needs to be changed in the way our schools involve their parents, train their teachers, test their students, teach their children, and spend their money. By focusing a clearer eye on these five areas—and by emulating those men and women who have brought excellence out of some of the worst conditions imaginable—we can gain valuable lessons for improving the performance of all schools in America.

PARENTAL ACCOUNTABILITY
Extending the mission of the school to the home

Today, a lack of parental involvement is often the first excuse for a school's poor performance. But high-performing principals have found that where academic achievement is the norm, parental support is not far behind.

"All low-performing schools have one thing in common," says Wilma Rimes, the principal who succeeded the legendary Thaddeus Lott at Wesley Elementary in Houston. "They allow too many things to disrupt classroom instruction. Well, parents can be the most disruptive of all. What you want is parents to help with a child's learning."

The point is that a school will not be improved simply by adding parents to the mix. As Rimes suggests, a well-run school might even be hindered by them. Above all else, effective principals want parents who are *personally invested* in the education of their children.

"Public education—inner-city education—is marked by disenfranchised parents," says Ernestine Sanders, the president of the Cornerstone Schools Association, a collection of privately owned, Christ-centered schools in Detroit. "The school has to bring about a transformation of attitude. A successful school is marked by parents committed to academic excellence." It helps in Cornerstone's case that parents have voluntarily chosen to send their children there, but sometimes even that is not enough. For Sanders, it is the *school's job* to ensure strong parental commitment.

Principals of high-performing schools want parents who value education and who will instill in their children the values that make for success in the classroom. Many high-performing principals realize that these values are not firmly in place at home, so they *establish contracts* with parents to support their child's efforts to learn.

Many of the schools studied here use a written contract signed by parents, teachers, and students alike. Most of these contracts:

- Outline the school's mission and state the non-negotiables.
- Demand high academic achievement for all.
- Clearly explain the school's expectations regarding:
  —parental responsibilities.
  —academic standards.
  —conduct and misconduct.
- Outline the penalties for non-compliance.
- Command the assent of all signatories.

"We state our expectations and let the parents know that if these things are not met, their child will lose privileges," says David Levin of the KIPP Academy in the Bronx. "If these things continue not to be met, the child will be asked to leave." KIPP in the Bronx is a neighborhood school that cannot legally expel a student, but no one has yet called Levin's bluff. Every parent knows there are five children on the KIPP waiting list for every child in the school.

"The contract establishes our expectations," Levin explains. "Parents want consistency. The contract does that. Parents get so many mixed messages from all the other schools. Our contract tells them that we hold everyone to the same high standard."

At the Cornerstone Schools in Detroit parents, teachers, and students sign what the schools call a "covenant." "In the covenant we identify the things we're responsible for," says Sanders. In her experience, it keeps the school on track, but more importantly, it lets the parents know that *the school* wants the parents to be close observers of its progress. "In the end, the covenant keeps the parents focused and the school focused," she says. "It helps the parents to ask the right questions of us, and it keeps the school answering to its mission."

KIPP, for example, has a no-fighting policy. Because of the contract, if a child fights at KIPP, he knows he may be suspended. "With that expectation in mind, we can talk to the student, we can talk to his parents and work out what's best for everyone," Levin remarks. "It helps us protect our standards. It's the ultimate guarantee of what we stand for."[4]

After stating obligations and expectations through the contract, high-performing schools give constant feedback to their families in other ways.

"Every school should have some means of updating parents *weekly*," Levin notes. "At a bare minimum parents need to know about their child's behavior, schoolwork, homework, and attendance."

At KIPP, both in Houston and in the Bronx, the school keeps parents informed through its system of student "paychecks," which also acts as a powerful motivator of enhanced student performance. Each week teachers evaluate their students in ten specific areas of performance ranging from personal neatness to the quality of their prepared assignments. Awarding up to $2 in each area, teachers send the children home with a weekly paycheck worth $0 to $20, which acts as a quick report on that week's activities. Once the check is endorsed with a parent's signature it is redeemable at the school store for books, supplies, CDs and other goods, appropriately sold at hyper-inflated prices. A CD might cost over $100 in KIPP cash, for example. KIPP paychecks thus notify the parents

Notes:

4. KIPP, Cornerstone, and many other high-performing schools studied in these pages emphasize policies and procedures reminiscent of practices long associated with the most effective Catholic schools. A clearly written handbook enforced by a no-nonsense contract is the best way to guarantee and gain from effective parental involvement, says Sister Helen Strueder, principal of Holy Angels School in Chicago, the largest black Catholic school in the country. At Holy Angels students are charged $1 for coming late to school and *their parents* are charged $15 if a child's homework is consistently incomplete. "We want our parents to help their children—this is one way to get their attention," she adds. "The change in society is the biggest problem we face," Sister Helen remarks. "You cannot impact the child without impacting the family first." All parents at Holy Angels agree to attend Mass every week, or monthly if they are non-Catholics; attend parent/teacher meetings each month; attend a year-long course in religious instruction; agree to the discipline code of the school; and agree to withdraw their child from the school voluntarily if they violate the terms of this contract.

of a child's weekly progress and give every child, every week, another reason to excel. If ever a parent or a child has a question, teachers at KIPP are available 24 hours a day by toll-free numbers that ring to their personal cellphones.

"We want to set the students up for success," says Michael Feinberg, the co-founder and director of the KIPP Academy in Houston. "Everything they need they can buy at the school store with their paycheck money. There's no excuse if they're unprepared. And their parents are told exactly what their children need to work on." Feinberg notes as an aside that the paychecks system also employs a number of students as bankers and accountants who learn further lessons in mathematics, economics, proper business practice, and honesty.

At George Washington Elementary in Chicago, parents turn to the student handbook to a daily planner that shows—subject by subject—how their child is moving through the curriculum. Subject assignments are recorded in the agenda every day. Craig Ergang, the principal at Washington, also mandates teacher contact with the parents every week. Every five weeks the school produces a mini-report card. And every ten weeks the school hosts an open house where the five-week notice is collected in person by the parents. If that isn't enough contact, there is a homework hotline for every grade level, every day.

High-performing principals teach parents to read to their children, check their homework, and ask after their assignments. Again, the focus has to be on academic achievement.

Many of the principals profiled in this book interview parents before the start of the school year. Others administer final exams to them at the year's end. Gregory Hodge of the Frederick Douglass Academy in New York says a parent only has to take one exam to learn the importance of checking homework regularly. At Cornerstone, homework is assigned four days a week and must come back every day signed by a parent.

Strict parental accountability in the early years is one of the most effective tools at a principal's disposal. High-performing principals tell parents of kindergartners months in advance what their child needs to know before school starts. For example, in June, Irwin Kurz used to give the parents of kindergartners at P.S. 161 in New York a copy of a test their children would take the following September. He then would go over the test and tell the parents how they could work with their children to prepare for school over the summer. This one practice allowed Kurz to identify with some accuracy the level of learning that takes place in the home. For those who struggle, Kurz had one of his Title I early childhood teachers teach the parents what to do to assist their child's effort in school. At George Washington Elementary, Ergang provides a training session for the parents of preschoolers designed to encourage more effective learning in the home.

Where necessary, high-performing schools often provide or recommend a literacy program for parents. For Vivian Dillihunt of Rozelle Elementary in Memphis, parental accountability is about two things: assisting students with their schoolwork and reinforcing the value of a child's formal education. Her school holds parenting workshops to increase parental literacy and to improve parents' ability to instruct their children at home. She and every high-performing principal in these pages say that parents of elementary school students should explicitly teach phonics in the home—a focus on reading at home is good for parents and students alike.

A lack of parental involvement, however, is no excuse for a school's poor performance. In the end, *each student*, not a child's parents, must be held accountable for his own individual success. "We let our children understand that so many opportunities are available even if their parents can't or won't help," says Hellen DeBerry, the former principal of Earhart Elementary in Chicago. "We talk a lot about the future, about good role models, and about careers. A school environment of achievement itself removes many obstacles." If a school fosters a clear culture of achievement, a parent need only reinforce the clear mission of the school. Effective parental participation, therefore, begins and ends with strong leadership in the school.

"Schools that are not performing well will never achieve parental support and do not deserve it either," Levin concludes. "The only thing you can do to earn parents' support is to educate their children."

TEACHERS
What to look for, where to find them, how to hire, how to fire

The inadequate training of teachers is the single most debilitating force at work in American classrooms today. Overcoming this failure is perhaps the single greatest accomplishment of high-performing, high-poverty schools.

"We need an entirely new teaching workforce," says David Levin of the KIPP Academy in the South Bronx. "Teachers today are like green paint. It's hard to get the blue out once the yellow has been mixed in. There are some great teachers out there, but they've been mixed among a bad element for too long."

Teachers at KIPP are in school during the week from 7:30 A.M. to 5:00 P.M., four hours on Saturday, and for two months during the summer. Yet KIPP has no difficulty attracting good teachers. As Mike Wallace reported in a recent episode of *60 Minutes*, many teachers leave their posts in other public schools and come to KIPP precisely because they want to be a part of a school that works—no matter what the demands are. "We put in 60, 70, 80-hour weeks here," says Josh Zoia, a science teacher at KIPP in New York. "I was doing that in my old school and it wasn't working. I was driving myself crazy. Here you put those hours in and *look what happens*."[5]

All high-performing schools make it their professional obligation to improve the daily course of instruction, because whatever else needs to happen to improve academic outcomes, teacher quality has to improve first. As William Sanders of the University of Tennessee has demonstrated, teacher quality is the single most accurate indicator of a student's educational attainment.[6]

Echoing Levin's earlier remark, high-performing principals maintain that, given today's pool of candidates, we can only staff a fraction of our nation's schools with people who are good enough to get the job done.[7] High-poverty schools have the hardest time of all attracting qualified teachers.[8]

"Teachers who are themselves discipline problems, low-performing, or otherwise unhireable are willing to work in hostile conditions and for poor pay, not because they are missionaries—but because they are des-

Notes:

5. *60 Minutes*, "KIPP," September 19, 1999.
6. See William L. Sanders and June C. Rivers, *Cumulative and Residual Effects of Teachers on Future Student Academic Achievement*, University of Tennessee Value-Added Research and Assessment Center, 1996.
7. A good deal of recent research backs this claim. Among high-school students who took the SAT in 1994-1995, those who intended to study education in college scored lower on both the verbal and math sections than students expressing an interest in any other field. (Thomas D. Snyder, *et al.*, *Digest of Education Statistics 1997*, U.S. Department of Education, p. 135.) In 1998 the mean SAT score for students who intended to major in education was 479 math and 485 verbal—32 and 20 points lower than all college-bound seniors. (Tyce Palmaffy, "Measuring the Teacher Quality Problem," in *Better Teachers, Better Schools*, edited by Marci Kanstoroom and Chester E. Finn, Jr., Thomas B. Fordham Foundation, pp. 21-22.) According to another study, once in college, education majors were more likely to be in the bottom quartile and less likely to be in the top quartile than any other major. (Robin R. Henke, *et al.*, *Out of the Lecture Hall and into the Classroom: 1992-1993 College Graduates and Elementary/Secondary School Teaching*, U.S. Department of Education, p. 58.)

perate," says Gregory Hodge of the Frederick Douglass Academy in Harlem. "You can see this wherever there are failing schools. The Board of Education in New York City selectively identified schools that it made dumping grounds based on geography and economics."

Ironically, good teachers are a rare commodity in great demand and yet no system is in place to supply that need or encourage a greater number of qualified applicants. Over the past thirty-five years the increased demand for teachers has actually diluted teacher quality, while the supply of qualified candidates has been undercut by the greater pay and prestige associated with other professions.

Many of the principals included in this study blame much of this system-wide failure on our nation's schools of education. To begin with, the teacher certification process discourages many potential candidates and positively bars the admission of many others who might otherwise be attracted to teaching. But more importantly, the actual content of so much teacher training is not directed to improving teacher performance. "You ought to shut down many, many schools of education," says Nancy Ichinaga of Bennett-Kew Elementary in Inglewood, California.

"Teachers coming from university teacher preparation programs do not know how to teach reading," says Thaddeus Lott, the former principal of Wesley Elementary in Houston. "When a first-year teacher comes to Wesley Elementary it then becomes the responsibility of the administration on the campus to train them. They must be taught what and how to teach. They must also learn how to manage a classroom. I have found that alternative teacher preparation programs, such as the Houston Independent School District Alternative Certification Program, produce much more competent and effective teachers," he remarks.

Charter schools in many states are not required to hire people who pass through schools of education or who are state certified. In this environment, well-educated adults can enter into teaching without first dawdling in expensive programs unrelated to their daily assignments as teachers. Tom Williams of Healthy Start Academy in North Carolina has no certified teachers among his faculty; he trains them all himself. "Teachers who can't make it are invited to leave around November," he

Notes:

8. Richard Ingersoll of the University of Georgia has studied teacher quality in America from a number of different angles. One representative finding: in high-poverty high schools, 43 percent of math teachers neither majored nor minored in a math-related field of study. That same statistic is 20 percentage points lower in wealthier districts. (Richard M. Ingersoll, "The Problem of Underqualified Teachers in American Secondary Schools," *Educational Researcher*, March 1999.)

says. Those who survive are paid $10,000 more than teachers in the local public schools and, what is more, are trained to produce results in the classroom.

Against this way of thinking, the education establishment is overly concerned with teacher credentials as opposed to teacher effectiveness. In policy arguments this is discussed as a focus on "inputs" (do teachers have the right diploma?) rather than "outcomes" (can their students make the grade?). For Tom Williams, this situation has created an industry that is perversely centered on the job stability of adults and not the learning of their students. "What you need is a teaching workforce willing to work for incentives. Good schools just can't afford to hold on to bad teachers," he concludes.

But good teachers are in short supply. Williams and other high-performing principals find that they either have to scour the earth or take what teachers they can and train them themselves.

"You don't just hire a teacher, you hire a particular skill set that you're looking for," says Gregory Hodge. "Teachers don't come to the Frederick Douglass Academy to retire. They come here to make a contribution. So I ask them: Will they make the time, will they sacrifice their other commitments, do they have the skills, do they bring the extra-curricular activities we need? If you really want quality, you simply have to keep interviewing until you find a match."

Hodge says that he looks longer and harder for his teachers than any other principal in his district. "We spend approximately seven months a year trying to recruit teachers," says Hodge. "I'll interview 100 to 150 teachers before I make a decision to hire." Hellen DeBerry says that most principals, for whatever reason, simply do not look hard enough. She searched on the Internet, went to job fairs, posted openings at career counseling offices across the country, and hand-picked teachers throughout the system. By the time DeBerry had effected Chicago's single most successful turn-around effort at Earhart Elementary, she had replaced nearly the entire school staff.

High school principals have to look for a very particular skill set—with a premium placed on expertise in a specific field. Among elementary and middle school principals, the number one thing they look for in a new teacher is desire—a love of learning and a love of children. In high-performing schools, where the culture of achievement is clearly articulated and the curriculum neatly mapped out, new teachers with these characteristics almost invariably succeed in their first year of teaching.

Without exception, high-performing principals consider themselves the instructional leaders of their schools. Principals or headmasters have to be just that—the lead teacher—and primarily so they can find or train other teachers to imitate their success. "If you were not a good teacher yourself, then you don't know what a good teacher looks like," says Hellen DeBerry, "and you certainly won't be a good principal if you can't find good teachers."

Irwin Kurz, the former principal of The Crown School, agrees and says that investing time in the interview process pays off. "A school is only as good as its staff, so you have to get the best available," he says. "In the inner city, a lot of principals are happy just not to have lousy teachers. But you need great teachers if you want your school to go anywhere. You either have to find them or teach them yourself."

Kurz's point is reiterated by successful principals throughout the country. It is so hard to find teachers with the right skills, it is often a better bet to find people with the right attitude. "A good school can make good people into good teachers," says Mary Kojes of P.S. 122. "You have to have a lot of other things in place—a clearly defined curriculum for one—but you can shape good people into good teachers."

Vivian Dillihunt agrees. "We don't always get the best teachers," says the Memphis, Tennessee, principal. "We take what we get and turn them into the best teachers through training, teamwork, and mentoring."

Like so many other high-performing principals, Dillihunt emphasizes the importance of teamwork for her teachers. For this reason, many high-performing principals select their new teachers by engaging their current staff in the interview process. Above all else this process identifies the team players and promotes a positive working chemistry among the faculty.

Team teachers also work to move out those teachers who don't have the vision or the commitment. "Bad teachers do not stay at Rozelle," says Dillihunt, who has been the principal there for five years. "Peer pressure causes those who do not want to succeed to leave." When a school's culture reveals who fits and who doesn't, outstanding principals say they have fewer fights with substandard teachers who are just trying to hold down a job.

Cooperation and teamwork may create a more collegial teaching environment and weed out bad apples, but a pleasant experience for the faculty is not the primary objective of this coordinated effort. Teamwork, with a keen focus on master teachers, is the key to ongoing staff development.

At P.S. 161, Irwin Kurz instituted a peer review system designed exclusively to share best practices within his building and to enhance the overall level of teaching in the classroom. Within this system, classroom teachers observe other classroom teachers at least three times a year. Kurz didn't read the peer review files that resulted—they were strictly for the teachers' internal use. At Frederick Douglass, new teachers have to observe *every* teacher in the building each semester, regardless of discipline. Similar to the peer review at P.S. 161, twice a year at KIPP every teacher receives a written profile of other teachers' observations. And every week a full-time staff developer visits every teacher.

This last practice of having a full-time staff developer on board seems to be taking hold among high-performing schools. Although in many districts the staff developer acts as a front man for an endless array of disconnected prepackaged training programs, many high-performing schools turn to a single staff developer to guarantee a certain quality of training and to enforce a certain uniformity of practice. Among high-performing elementary schools it is most common to see reading specialists act as full-time staff developers who enforce the school's long-term academic objectives.

At other schools it is the principal who performs this job. For example, at Marcus Garvey and at Marva Collins, two of the longest-running and most successful private efforts to educate low-income children, the founders of each school are still involved in the regular staff development of their teachers. "Teaching inabilities are as prevalent as learning disabilities," Marva Collins says. To this day, at both schools, it is the primary job of the principal to provide for and monitor the ongoing training of their teachers.

Above all else, high-performing schools use the hiring and firing of staff to communicate the ideals of their mission.

"In my final interview with the candidate, I lay down the law," says Hodge. "As quickly as you're hired, you can be fired. If you don't perform—you're gone." At this point Hodge says certain candidates get squeamish and ask how they will be evaluated. "How will you evaluate your students? Through test scores," Hodge replies. "That's how I'll evaluate you—through *their* test scores."

"My success is that I minimize the miscreants," says Hodge. "You can waste so much time getting rid of bad teachers it is better never to hire them." Hodge notes that if a teacher is failing the school, it is the principal's duty to try to improve that teacher's performance. But sometimes, in order to protect the children, a teacher simply has to go.

All across the country it is simply too difficult and too costly to get rid of a bad teacher. Typically in this process the principal has to recommend all firings to the superintendent who then recommends the same to the local school board. The district's evaluation plan—usually first approved by the state—has to be carefully followed in order for a firing to be successfully executed. All in all, four or five layers of decision-making power separate the incompetent teacher from the final authority capable of removing him.

Not surprisingly, many high-performing principals attribute some portion of their success to their ability to unload low-performing staff. Most of them say that their colleagues who can't negotiate the subtleties of union contracts or who are unable to maintain detailed personnel files simply have to suffer teachers who they know are hurting their school.

James Coady, principal of Morse Elementary in Cambridge, Massachusetts, recommends that all teachers be hired as "extended term substitutes" for the first year. In the event that a teacher is not a good fit with the school, the substitute teacher's contract can be terminated without any interference from the union. But he finds that a loyal staff can best separate the wheat from the chaff. "The teachers will work together to move a bad teacher out," Coady says.

Craig Ergang of George Washington Elementary in Chicago is quick to note that teachers need protection from power-hungry principals who might wreak havoc if teachers had no recourse to due process. But in his own school, performance is what matters. What does he do with someone who won't respond to the usual incentives?

"Take the 8th grade teacher and stick him in kindergarten. He'll find other opportunities," he replies.

TESTING
Diagnosis is not discrimination

For years standardized achievement tests have been used as a neutral measurement of academic performance. Yet, throughout their history both the objectivity of these exams and their ability to assess meaningful differences in educational attainment have been called into question. If one race, class, or gender regularly outperforms others, the tests are said to have a disparate impact on certain groups, making the tests themselves discriminatory. Going a bit further, opponents of standardized tests even claim there is an *inevitability* to the results—rich children do well while the poor score poorly, for example—making the official use of these exams positively dangerous and their authoritative acceptance in accountability programs only a tool of further division. Still other critics object to what they derisively call "teaching to the test," claiming that standardized tests are no test at all, but merely a gimmick that both feigns real achievement and stifles higher-order thinking.

Almost without exception, the high-performing principals in this study strongly reject this view.

"If the achievement scores at the end of the year show bad results, that's not the test's fault. That shows lousy teaching," says Tom Williams, headmaster of Healthy Start Academy, a public charter school in Durham, North Carolina. "The point is what you do with the results, not the excuses you make to cover for them."

Williams, like other supporters of standardized testing, says he values the test results because they enable him to benchmark his school's yearly progress and compare his local program against a national standard. "We're serious about the national exams because we want to publicize our achievement," Williams says decisively. For the second year in a row his elementary school, which is 99 percent black and 80 percent low-income, has had whole grade levels scoring in the nation's top 1 percent on the Iowa Test of Basic Skills (ITBS).

But to get these results, Williams says, a school has to stand behind the tests as a diagnostic tool that can effectively drive student achievement. For example, two years ago, Healthy Start's 1st graders scored in the 48th percentile on the ITBS. In response to this unacceptable result, their teachers threw out their curriculum and focused exclusively on math and reading for the entire year. In 1999, the same children, now in the 2nd grade, scored in the 99th percentile in all subjects.

Yet, across the country, national exams continue to spark violent opposition because the test scores from certain groups continue to show a hopeless lack of learning. Williams maintains that whatever racial disparity might be present in the test scores is not due to the tests themselves. "Discrimination is in the teaching, not in the testing," Williams says. "You either believe your children can learn—and you give the test to prove it—or you don't." He continues, "We understand the difficulties our children deal with in the community and at home, but we refuse to victimize them further by making excuses for them."

In support of Williams's point, anti-test prejudice is singularly absent from high-performing schools, regardless of their student make-up. "We take the national exams because I want my hand reaching out to all 50 states," says Ernest Smith, principal of Portland Elementary. "I want our children to know they can compete in Alaska as well as in Arkansas."

Smith is the principal of a small rural school in the Mississippi Delta region of Arkansas that five years ago was providing a substandard education to just about every child that walked through its doors. "Most of the children were reading two or three years below grade level, but the school had no idea how poorly it was doing," Smith says candidly. "Now every teacher is aware of the national percentile ranking of every one of her students. Needless to say, the difference shows." Although they number only nine students, this year's 6^(th) graders—who have been at Portland the five years Smith has been at the helm—scored in the 72^(nd) percentile in reading and 84^(th) in math.

"You hear this malarkey that the tests are designed for middle-class white kids," Smith continues. "We don't see that here." Nearly eight out of ten children at Portland come from low-income families. Thirty-five percent of Portland students are black.

According to many high-performing principals, the current trend to eliminate testing altogether, as an element in the national debate over affirmative action, is completely misguided. Although positive results on a national exam alone do not demonstrate a school's complete worth, the diagnostic function of such testing is an essential element of any school's planned success. More to the point, standardized tests should be just *one aspect* of a regular regime of rigorous testing.

"The more you test, the better the students do," says David Levin of the KIPP Academy in the Bronx. "Regardless of what teaching style you use, there has to be a constant assessment in place that demonstrates real mastery of what you are teaching."

High-performing principals all across the nation echo Levin's comment. "We believe in testing, because you need proof of a child's mastery," says Nancy Ichinaga, principal of Bennett-Kew Elementary in Inglewood, California. "No test is perfect. True. No test reveals the whole child. True. But I just want to make the child literate and testing is a necessary part of that process."

If Ichinaga sounds slightly exasperated—she is. For over twenty-five years she has had to buck nearly every trend in elementary education in order to guarantee the success of her students. But the modern-day resistance to testing she condemns as positively anti-intellectual. "Every profession uses objective measures to determine effectiveness. Educators don't like the results of their tests, so they condemn the measure. But only a poor workman quarrels with his tools."

And this comes from a woman who once had reason to quarrel with the results. When Nancy Ichinaga started at what was then Bennett Elementary in 1974, her school taken as a whole tested at the 3^(rd) percentile on the state exam in reading. "I told my teachers, 'Either all of our students are retarded or you don't know how to teach,'" she recounts. "But from that day on we learned to take responsibility for our students' learning." For over twenty years now, Ichinaga's school has been among the highest performing in all of Los Angeles County. Regular assessments, she says, are a key element to her school's successful academic record. "If you don't test, you won't know what to teach—it's as simple as that," she concludes.

Like Ichinaga, Ernest Smith has built his school around a regular routine of testing. "We believe that if the learner has not learned, the teacher has not taught," Smith declares plainly. "All children, when placed at their appropriate instructional level, can learn. If a child is not successful in school, the teacher and administration must accept responsibility for that failure and re-teaching must occur." In other words, the instructional program itself has to be aligned with a sequence of assessments that report on the regular progress of the students. At Portland Elementary, mastery tests are given every ten lessons, that is, every seven or eight days students can expect individual assessments in reading, language, math, and spelling.

Portland's emphasis on basic skills is another regular feature of high-performing, high-poverty schools. And wherever basic skills are preached, rigorous and regular testing is invariably a part of the mix.

"There's no point trying to teach a child if you are above him or below him," says Tom Williams of Healthy Start. Williams describes his school as a "diagnostic prescriptive school," that is, his school provides a personalized educational program for each child based on a careful assessment of that student's individual needs. Once a child is properly placed in the school, frequent curriculum-based assessments track the child's progress and accelerate his learning through the program based on his performance. Williams says it is through a regular regime of testing that difficulties of any kind are most easily identified, remediated, and corrected. "We use tests to figure out the problems, fix them, and move on," he says. And even when there *aren't* problems *testing* keeps both the curriculum and the instructional level right on target.

Thaddeus Lott, the former principal of Wesley Elementary in Houston, says that school discipline can also be dramatically improved by keeping a close eye on test results. "Disruptive and disobedient children are either bored or frustrated," he says. "The easiest way to maintain order in a school is to teach to everyone's appropriate instructional level. But you just can't do that without a data-driven approach to school management. You have to expect a lot and test a lot to get a lot."

Interestingly, this same observation extends to some children who are inappropriately placed in special education classes. "Many children are not *academically* deficient but *behaviorally* deficient," Lott says. "Unfortunately, their behavior problems are never addressed and they wind up being non-readers and not succeeding. This can be avoided through better diagnosis. The same thing happens to some slow learners. They get labeled Special Ed., but a better school, with better diagnostic testing, would find their appropriate instructional level, and teach to it with greater success."

Testing clearly has its limits. In particular, standardized tests serve very specific purposes that must not be overextended if they are to be used well. But high-performing principals say you cannot run an effective school if you are scared of test results. In short, a resistance to testing reveals a fear of poor performance. "It's just another excuse," says Al Jessie of Cascade Elementary in Atlanta. "They say they know the children will fail, so don't test them. Fact is—*they're* the ones who've failed."

BASIC SKILLS
How progressive education has hurt low-income children most of all

Typically in America, the longer a child is in the public school system the worse he performs. As is well known in education circles, American 12th graders now rank dead last among industrial nations in math and science.[9] Regardless of race, class, or family background, we are losing too many children to school failure and low achievement.

According to many high-performing principals, much of this failure is the result of reckless educational theories that have nothing to do with the way children learn. "We were all terrible failures coming out of our teachers' colleges," says Nancy Ichinaga, "because the children didn't behave the way we were told they should."

In general, Ichinaga believes that child psychology has replaced basic skills and a therapeutic culture has replaced a culture of achievement. "They're all Freudians!" she says, referring to the regnant educational theorists. "But a teacher is more of a scientist. You build from the inside out. Nothing is assumed in our method. We know what to look for and we check it off as we go. That's why we believe in testing. We want proof."

"Educators pour all of their energy into cognition studies, but they don't know how students learn," Ichinaga says. "They have all these great big *Gestalt* theories that don't work. Human beings don't learn that way. They learn in bits."

High-performing principals know that children need to be taught basic skills in a sequence that logically builds from the most elementary foundations to increasingly higher-order conceptual thinking. They

Notes:
9.   See *http://www.heritage.org/issues/chap9.html.*

maintain that a misguided rejection of basic skills has caused much of the failure in our classrooms today. Instead of learning how to teach, teachers are taught how children learn. And yet, much of this developmental psychology—when it is not fundamentally flawed—is of remarkably little use in the everyday task of teaching.

"Educators are all worried about how the whole child can fit into society," Ichinaga says. "The classroom should be like a family, they say. But they never talk about basic skills that need to be mastered or the proper sequence for teaching them most effectively."

E.D. Hirsch, Jr., author of *The Schools We Need and Why We Don't Have Them* and founder of the Core Knowledge Foundation, has already argued this point conclusively. Romantic notions of how children learn have skewed classroom instruction away from its proper grounding in the basic skills, which are the necessary preconditions of later learning. But Ichinaga and many other high-performing principals say that something even more virulent lies within this overall approach to teaching.

While the education establishment's rejection of basic skills in favor of "life-long learning" or "higher-order problem solving" originated as an effort to raise educational standards to new heights, in practice it has become an excuse to cover for present-day failure. So long as clearly measurable educational goals are denounced in favor of such ambiguous intellectual aspirations, children will not learn what they need to know and teachers will not be accountable to the needs of their students.

"Nothing basic should be dropped for something new down the pike," says Mary Kojes of P.S. 122. "Yes, I want our students to develop critical thinking, but they can't without content first." Or, as E.D. Hirsch, Jr. has put it so memorably: "There are no real-world examples of adults with information-age competencies who are functioning with a 4th-grade vocabulary."[10]

Only three high school programs appear in this study and all three of them grew out of their middle schools. High-performing principals say there are few excellent high schools serving low-income populations, primarily because basic skills are wanting in the grades below. In other words, high schools now have to remediate, because the earlier grades fail to educate. In high-performing high schools, however, basic skills are the gateway to the study of higher-order disciplines.

The basic skill *par excellence* is reading. All of the high-performing elementary schools studied here make reading in kindergarten a pri-

Notes:

10. E.D. Hirsch, Jr., *The Schools We Need and Why We Don't Have Them* (New York: Doubleday, 1996), p. 145.

mary objective—regardless of family background or secondary language. "I believe, and research supports, that when children are taught to read in kindergarten using a direct systematic approach, they are able to enter the 1st grade on the same level as their counterparts, no matter what their socioeconomic status," says Thaddeus Lott. E.D. Hirsch, Jr. has taken this point one step further: "Every child reading at grade level by the end of 1st or 2nd grade would do more than any other single reform to improve the quality and equity of American schooling."[11]

Many educational theorists who stress a cognitive skills approach would disagree with this position. They promote a "child-centered" model intended to develop verbal skills based on a child's own self-directed process.[12] For them, low-income children are often low-performing because their normal cognitive experiences are insufficient. They maintain that poor children come to school with fewer language experiences and less verbal ability and so should not be expected to complete the same level of work, or at least not in the same period of time. Lott retorts, "Children should be able to read at the end of the year you first started teaching them to read."

These same theorists have also pushed an affective skills model, in which the development of self-esteem is deemed essential to the acquisition of academic abilities. It is assumed that the child knows what is best for his personal growth and that he will not learn well unless he first feels good about his learning. By this way of thinking, a child grows into educational proficiency in a way that is "developmentally appropriate" for him. This model lets everyone off the hook. Not only does the teacher not have to teach, but also it is appropriate for certain children not to excel.

Whole language is the best known myth that has emerged from this mistake.

"Education schools talk about what is 'developmentally appropriate,' but reading is not developmental or natural. Reading is learned," say Nancy Ichinaga. According to Ichinaga, the end result of so much bogus educational theory is that children are knowingly left behind. And, if children fall behind when they are young, they necessarily fall further behind as time progresses, because reading is an ordered skill that builds on elementary components of previously learned material. "Adults with reading problems have the same difficulties as children

Notes:

11. *Ibid.*, p. 148.
12. Gary L. Adams and Siegfried Engelmann, *Research on Direct Instruction: 25 Years Beyond DISTAR* (Seattle: Educational Achievement Systems, 1996), p. 69.

with reading problems," she says. "Overcoming these problems is not a matter of outgrowing them."

Low-income children often suffer the most from these useless fads. Shifted from one program to another in a series of interventions that are sometimes at odds with each other, low-income children aren't taught as much as they are trial-tested. And, according to Tom Williams of Healthy Start Academy, many of these programs are just thrown at low-income schools in a desperate effort to hide the fact that they are failing.

Like many other high-performing principals, Williams knows what works and so he doesn't seek refuge in new-fangled theories. But what he finds shameful is the effort to bury failure in a shell game of jargon and doublespeak, which claims to identify a child's problem, but which is unequipped to improve his educational outcomes. "We don't fail our students before they begin by calling them 'at-risk,'" he says. "We teach them—however they come to us."

"The trouble is," says Irwin Kurz, the former principal of P.S. 161, "they're always trying to teach *these kids* in a different way because they're poor. Just teach them! They say they're trying to anticipate their needs, but what they do is determine their failure."

The soundest lesson that high-performing schools can teach is that all children require a basic set of skills in order to succeed in school. They need to listen attentively, speak persuasively, read with understanding, and write with command. Not all children acquire all of these skills solely in school, but they have to get them somewhere. As a result, higher-income children are often better able to withstand the inconsistencies of an experimental education because their home life provides learning opportunities not generally available to low-income children. An emphasis on basic skills, however, can guarantee that all children get what they need to succeed, regardless of family background.

DOLLARS AND SENSE
What principals spend their money on and why

More than anything else low-performing schools are said to need more money. No matter how poor they may be, no high-performing schools make this excuse. In fact, the spending habits of the No Excuses schools can be highly instructive for those who need to make a little go a long way.

"We ran KIPP from the first day like a business," Michael Feinberg remarks. He adds that many charter schools in particular are struggling because they failed to institute the right business practices from the start. Keen fiscal management is especially important in the charter school environment, he says, because under the current law no money is appropriated for capital expenses and the margin for error is so slim.

KIPP operates on a break-even basis, spending $5,650 per child per year. Of this, the school has to raise $850 per child in private donations each year to cover its capital expenses and the cost of its many additional programs. This compares to the average per pupil expenditure of $5,672 in Houston and $5,482 statewide.[13] It is important to note that KIPP does not spend less than most schools in Texas, but it does produce dramatically different results with no greater resources. Similarly, KIPP in New York is heavily dependent on private funding, but with no more money than its neighboring schools, KIPP's record of achievement puts the others to shame.

The actual practices of the No Excuses schools are rather varied: some contract out non-instructional services, as they do at Healthy Start. Some develop creative lend/leasing policies with neighboring schools or other local institutions, as they do at Cornerstone. Still others seek out public/private partnerships, as is increasingly becoming the norm for many charter schools. But one thing is true of all high-performing principals: they manage their money in an effort to *improve student performance*. In all high-performing schools—public, private, and parochial—student performance is the bottom line.

In general, effective principals spend their money on two things: their curricula and their teachers. Ironically, in the public school system, these are the two areas where the least spending flexibility is provided. Typically, materials for state-mandated curricula are supplied directly to the school and automatically billed against the school's budget. Similarly, teacher wages and compensation are dictated by union-negotiated collective bargaining agreements outside the local control of the school administration. For example, James Coady of the Morse School only has control over $29,000 within his school's $3-million budget. All the same, high-performing principals manage to supercharge both the content and the delivery of instruction in their schools by the way they spend the money that is within their jurisdiction.

Spending on curriculum generally falls into two categories: added instructional support and additional instructional materials. Support comes in many kinds. Many high-performing schools, such as Cornerstone and KIPP, have longer years and longer days. But most schools

Notes:

13. Provided by the Houston Independent School District.
    See *http://www.houstonisd.org.*

improve instruction by adding math, science, language arts, and history specialists who augment the curriculum, give it added features, broaden its content, and take it to a higher level. Among elementary and middle schools, reading specialists are the chief investment.

"I have always placed reading at the top of my list of financial priorities at Wesley," says Thaddeus Lott. For several years, Hellen DeBerry paid every adult at Earhart to teach reading. The P.E. instructor, the music teacher, the librarian, and everyone on the support staff learned to teach reading through DeBerry's expert guidance and a few outside professional development seminars. "You don't have to spend more money," DeBerry notes, "you have to rearrange your priorities. At a certain time each day we asked everybody to drop everything and teach reading. We only had to pay for their time."

Surprisingly, many high-performing, high-poverty schools have found that math and science can be done very well on the cheap. At Washington Elementary in Chicago, Craig Ergang combines his 7th and 8th grade classes in a life sciences/physical sciences program that alternates from year to year. At Earhart, also in Chicago, a rolling science lab that is stored in a closet moves from grade to grade. In elementary schools, a single math specialist, who moves from class to class supporting the regular teaching practices of the full-time classroom teachers, can make all the difference between a good and an outstanding math program. Alyson Barillari of Fourteenth Avenue in Newark explains, "For the price of one teacher, I can improve the teaching of everyone in the entire building." In fact, Barillari has expanded this zone-defense approach to professional development to cover all disciplines. "No one needs to leave the building for staff development," she adds.

Discussion of outside instructional support invariably raises the contentious issue of class size reduction, but high-performing principals are of mixed opinion on the cost effectiveness of this approach to improving student performance. Hellen DeBerry's experience at Earhart Elementary is a case in point: "In 1991 we had so few students, Chicago Public Schools was going to shut the school down. If class size were everything, we should have had terrific results. Every year since then our classes got bigger as our scores got better." This being said, Craig Ergang, DeBerry's colleague at a neighboring school, is quick to point out, "You can't let children hide. I reduce class size as much as possible in the primary grades, especially in the reading groups." Ergang's experience is common to many principals in these pages. While he is willing to pay for small, homogeneous reading groups in the early grades, he still has 33 and 32 children per class in grades 6 and 7.

Paying for outside instructional support, however, is most characteristic of whole school reform models. The paid consultants who advised on the implementation of Direct Instruction at Portland Elementary are a good example of this. Interestingly, the most successful schools that incur this expense are usually able to train their own once the model has successfully taken root. Portland Elementary and Wesley Elementary, for example, are now sources of Direct Instruction teachers and teacher training for schools in their local regions. Likewise, Rozelle Elementary is a national demonstration site for the Modern Red Schoolhouse design.

No one is settling for the inequity of underfunded schools, but the lesson taught by high-performing principals is how to get the most out of marginal expenditures. "It's not how much you have; it's how you spend it," says Mary Kojes. Tom Williams is a bit more explicit. "I never do anything myself that I can buy," he says, "I buy transportation, I buy food service, I buy accounting. But I'll tell you what I don't spend my money on. I don't spend my money on guidance counselors, psychologists, speech therapists, assistant principals or anyone else who does not deal directly with teaching the children." When necessary, Williams contracts out these non-essential services and finds ways to fund them that do not tax his general operating budget. Necessary speech services, for example, are paid for by Medicare.

Many principals who spend their discretionary funds on curriculum say that high-powered supplements are the way to go. "Children need difficult reading to keep them above grade level," says Craig Ergang. His school supplies this need through a modest learning center and a Junior Great Books program for the more advanced students in grades 2 through 8. Although most high-poverty schools need several years or outside grants to pull the money together, for $15,000 a school can acquire an 800-book library of the best in contemporary children's literature that is sufficient to meet the needs of all of its students. This is an essential investment for any school that hopes to improve educational outcomes. Even the poorest high-performing schools overflow with quality reading materials.

Music and the arts are also popular categories of discretionary spending. Craig Ergang maintains that any successful school has to invest in the arts. "Art is the key to success for so many students," he says. "For low-income children it exposes them to so much they would never get elsewhere." Ergang even pays his music teacher extra to assemble the band in the morning before school starts. At KIPP in New York, Rozelle in Memphis, and GAMP in Philadelphia, the arts comprise the largest component of the school's spending on instruction.

Principals who purchase additional instructional materials generally do so for two reasons: either they are forbidden to buy them through the usual funding channels, or they need them to execute alternative, accelerated, or advanced programs.

"*Reading Mastery* has never been on the State of Texas approved textbook list," says Thaddeus Lott. "*Reading Mastery* materials are costly, but since reading is a priority, purchasing an effective reading program takes precedence." Many principals even have to break the rules or otherwise devise creative accounting methods to purchase unapproved materials or additional materials not within their strict budgetary limits. The line-item for janitorial supplies, for example, is sometimes used to buy added textbooks: the principals simply report to the Central Office that they purchased "paper products."

This sad example makes an important point: in their own way, successful public schools act like charter schools. But while fiscal autonomy is a hallmark of charter schools, high-performing public schools have to fight for their financial freedom. Sometimes this freedom comes at great personal sacrifice. "We spend on the curriculum as much as possible," says Jim Coady of the Morse School. At Morse, the teachers know that the school receives $20,000 annually to reimburse substitute teachers. Whatever funds from this account that are not spent at the end of the year are reimbursed to the school for general use. As a result, teachers often come in sick so that the school can use the substitute teacher account to buy additional study materials for its Core Knowledge curriculum.

Consumable workbooks and advanced textbooks are often the most expensive of the supplementary materials. "Advanced Placement programs are expensive," says Gregory Hodge. "I have to offer AP courses in spite of the Board of Education—and I have to cut corners—because I don't receive any extra money for these added offerings. I think it's a disgrace that I have to cut corners to offer a curriculum that is more demanding and sure to create more opportunities for my students."

Principals are often forced to manipulate their budgets to their advantage because their budgets are not suited to meet their needs. "The Central Administration dictates our budget based on *projected*, not actual, demographics," says Jim Coady. By this system, the Morse School is actually *punished* for being a popular school that attracts new families to the area.

More generally, low-income schools (which often serve itinerant populations) are underfunded because they have high mobility rates, that is, large percentages of children who enter or leave the school in a given year. With many school budgets determined by October 1 or October

15 fiscal calendars, many schools are forced to make do with budgets that do not reflect the actual populations attending their schools by December. If, however, a certain level of funding followed the child to her school of choice, better schools would be better rewarded for their better performance. As these schools demonstrate, when low-income families are free to decide which schools they can attend, they go where the schooling is best.

Under the current laws guiding most public school districts, it is difficult for principals to tie their budgetary practice to teacher performance. Still, all of the schools in this study find ways of rewarding their teachers. A 15-percent salary increase at KIPP offsets the longer day, for example; but at Healthy Start, $10,000 more annually is designed to attract and reward a higher-performing teacher. "Eighty percent of every dollar that comes into Healthy Start goes into teachers' salaries," says Tom Williams. Healthy Start provides superior health insurance for its teachers and contributes 8 percent of a teacher's annual salary to individually managed retirement accounts. At the end of the year, merit-based bonuses range from $1,000 to $2,000 per teacher. "I have no trouble recruiting teachers," says Williams. "One third of my staff are male teachers because they can raise a family on what I pay them."

Where principals are not able to provide bonuses or performance pay, high-performing principals reward their teachers with individual staff development, whether through seminars, graduate study, or sabbaticals. "My job is to provide the best conditions possible for my teachers," says Irwin Kurz, reiterating a line more often repeated by high-performing principals than any other: "If they say they need it, I find a way to get it for them."

The No Excuses Schools

Ernest Smith
Portland Elementary, Portland, AR

Nancy Ichinaga
Bennett-Kew Elementary, Inglewood, CA

Vanessa Beverly
Marcus Garvey School, Los Angeles, CA

Alfonso L. Jessie, Jr.
Cascade Elementary, Atlanta, GA

Cynthia Collins
Marva Collins Preparatory School, Chicago, IL

Hellen DeBerry
Earhart Elementary, Chicago, IL

Craig Ergang
George Washington Elementary, Chicago, IL

James Coady
Morse Elementary, Cambridge, MA

Ernestine Sanders
Cornerstone Schools Association, Detroit, MI

Patsy Burks
Owen Elementary, Detroit, MI

Ronald Williams
Newberry Elementary, Detroit, MI

Alyson Barillari
Fourteenth Avenue School, Newark, NJ

Irwin Kurz
P.S.161—The Crown School, Brooklyn, NY

Mary Kojes
P.S. 122—The Mamie Fay School, Long Island City, NY

Gregory Hodge
Frederick Douglass Academy, New York, NY

David Levin
KIPP Academy, Bronx, NY

Thomas E. Williams
Healthy Start Academy, Durham, NC

Angelo F. Milicia
Stephen Girard / GAMP, Philadelphia, PA

Vivian C. Dillihunt
Rozelle Elementary, Memphis, TN

Michael Feinberg
KIPP Academy, Houston, TX

Wilma B. Rimes
Mabel B. Wesley Elementary, Houston, TX

Across the country, dozens of schools with high concentrations of low-income children are proving that poverty is not the cause of academic failure. All of the No Excuses schools have a building-wide median score at or above the 65th percentile on national achievement tests, even though 75 percent or more of their students qualify for the free or reduced-price lunch. By contrast, similar schools typically score below the 35th percentile.

The schools studied here are not necessarily the best high-poverty schools in the country; neither were they chosen from a definitive survey of outstanding low-income schools. No definitive list of high-performing, high-poverty schools can be assembled, because there is no single source for this kind of information. The annual surveys of America's "best" schools are more suggestive than they are authoritative. This report is no different.

Reliable test data are very hard to come by and are not necessarily comparable from year to year. Reporting procedures in different locales vary so greatly and achievement records are often presented so obscurely that it is difficult to identify real academic accomplishment. State tests are rarely comparable and so are of little use to a study of this kind. Finally, the many test exemptions associated with special education students, limited English proficiency, a child's housing status, and a myriad of other demographic considerations make it very difficult to identify a single body of students, in a single school, in a single year, who perform at a given level that can be said with certainty to be excellent and deserving of further study.

Obviously, many other excellent schools are not mentioned here. For one, there are hundreds of charter schools recently established in low-income areas that are doing well, but still have a way to go before becoming national success stories. There are also many magnet schools serving low-income children that also provide a first-rate education. But because magnets represent a form of public school choice, they are often far less residentially segregated than local public schools. Magnets hardly ever serve a student population that is disproportionately poor. There is an important lesson in this.

Several of the schools in this study experienced significant decreases in their percentage of low-income students after they improved academically. Their scores did not improve as a result of their poor students leaving. Rather, these case studies demonstrate that a high-performing school is attractive to all families regardless of race, income level, or family background.

One of the biggest surprises of this study is that no Catholic schools are represented. For years research has consistently demonstrated that inner-city Catholic schools outperform their local public school counterparts.[14] This report does not refute that finding; rather, the extraordinary achievement of Catholic schools is very different than the success criterion established for this study. While there are, particularly in the younger grades (K-4), a large number of low-income Catholic school students scoring in the top 25 percent of the country, their schools do not have building-wide median test scores at or above the 65th percentile or it is difficult to find reliable test data confirming their achievement.

A few things should be immediately apparent while reading these case studies. For one, these schools are different and their differences are clearly an important part of their strength. Secondly, the men and women who run these schools are the kinds of leaders and educational entrepreneurs that America needs more of, if we are to repair our system of education—especially for low-income children. And thirdly, the record of achievement established in these schools raises the bar on *every* school in the country that has more resources or is located in a less hostile environment.

In other words, these schools are a foretaste of what choice and competition would bring to education in America. These case studies demonstrate that given the freedom that they've long lost to bureaucracies, teachers' unions, and a hopeless degree of regulation, our schools today possess the intelligence, the inventiveness, and the willpower to compete.

Notes:

14. Most recently see Kirk A. Johnson, *Comparing Math Scores of Black Students in D.C.'s Public and Catholic Schools*. The Heritage Foundation (No. 99-08), October 1999.

Ernest Smith

Portland Elementary
314 Highway 278 E
Portland, AR 71663
870.737.4333

Portland Elementary has a lesson to teach the entire nation. In the past three years more than 60 groups of educators from 33 districts across four states have come to this school to learn from its methods. What they take away is a clear and concise lesson in the priority of basic skills.

Located in a remote region of the Mississippi Delta farm country—more than an hour-and-a-half drive from the nearest airport in Monroe, Louisiana—Portland is a rural town of fewer than 600 people who make their living working cotton fields, bean fields, and catfish farms.

When Ernest Smith came to Portland five years ago, half of the students in the 4th, 5th, and 6th grades were scoring two years or more below grade level. Today, 100 percent of the school is at grade level or above and improving 5 percentile points annually. In 1999 both the 1st and 2nd graders scored in the 78th percentile on the math portion of the Stanford-9. The 6th graders scored in the 72nd percentile in reading and 84th in math.[16]

"I tell the school the 100th percentile is our goal," says Smith.

With the desegregation of the public schools in 1970, white students in the surrounding area fled to private schools. Portland's academic success is now reversing that trend. Now 65 percent of Portland Elementary is white, 100 percent of the school-age children in its attendance zone are enrolled, and every month Smith gets more requests to transfer children to his school.

Grades: PK-6
Students: 152
% Low-income: 77
Median Percentile in Reading: 59
Median Percentile in Math: 66[15]

Direct Instruction has been a key element in this turnaround (see Appendix A). Known in the 1960s as DISTAR, Direct Instruction (DI) is a highly structured teaching method that has met with great success accelerating the learning of "at-risk" students. "DI has taught us that all

Notes:

15. Stanford-9 Achievement Test, Spring 1999. Provided by Portland Elementary.
16. *Ibid.*

children, when placed at their appropriate instructional level, can learn," says Smith. "We believe that, if the learner has not learned, the teacher has not taught."

In this very specific form of teaching, students are placed in small homogeneous groups by skill level. If mastery is not achieved at each stage of study, the material is re-taught and re-tested until every child in the group is at mastery. In this scheme, the focus on testing is designed to assess minute degrees of skill level in order to drive further achievement. At Portland Elementary, mastery tests are given every ten lessons, that is, every seven or eight days students can expect individual assessments in reading, language, math, and spelling.

Inspired in large part by Thaddeus Lott and the extraordinary success of Direct Instruction at Wesley Elementary in Houston, Smith and his teachers made a five-year commitment to J/P Associates, a consulting firm from New York that first trained the staff on DI's fast-paced, call-and-response, scripted approach to learning. After the initial training, coaches from J/P then came monthly to monitor all the teachers and correct their techniques where necessary. "The first year of the program is pretty tough on the teachers," Smith admits, "but none would go back now."

What thus began as a remediation program is now the center of Portland's curriculum, providing the school with a clear academic focus, ongoing staff development, rigorous student assessment, and a culture of learning that is infecting the region with its success. About 30 schools have implemented DI after visiting Portland Elementary. Without adopting DI statewide, the entire state of Arkansas has recently imitated the Portland approach by concentrating on basic skills and by restricting its PK–2nd grade curriculum to reading, language, spelling, and math.

"I've been 41 years in this business, 24 as a school principal, and the last five have been the best of my career," Smith reminisces. "We're so proud of these youngsters, I have no intention of retiring anytime soon."

Nancy Ichinaga

Bennett-Kew
Elementary School
11710 Cherry Avenue
Inglewood, CA 90303
310.680.5400

When Nancy Ichinaga became principal of Andrew Bennett Elementary in 1974, 95 percent of the children in her school were illiterate. In only four years she raised the school-wide reading performance from the 3rd to the 50th percentile in the state of California. After that, achievement kept on climbing, and for 20 years her school has been one of the highest performers in all of Los Angeles County. A mastery of reading in kindergarten is one of the keys to her success.

"As elementary school teachers," Ichinaga says, "our primary mission is to make children literate." Ichinaga has stuck to the principles she and her staff agreed upon in 1974. They determined that they needed a good reading program that had a systematic decoding component. In addition, they needed a teaching method that would make all children accountable and responsible learners beginning in the earliest years.

Beginning in kindergarten, all children in her school are taught to read and write English and are promoted according to clearly defined standards of achievement per grade level. Even kindergartners are held back if they don't meet the promotion requirement. "One of our most successful interventions has been to require kindergartners to know all the letter sounds and to be able to blend three letters to read words," Ichinaga explains. The neediest kindergartners are given an extra year before 1st grade to guarantee from the beginning that promotion is tied to achievement. "These children generally become successful 1st graders the following year," Ichinaga notes, "thereby preventing any cycle of school failure from beginning."

Grades: K-5
Students: 836
% Low-income: 78
Median Percentile in Reading: 62
Median Percentile in Math: 74[17]

The school is now bringing additional firepower to kindergarten in the form of the Waterford Early Reading Program, a multi-media sup-

Notes:

17. Stanford-9 Achievement Test, Spring 1999. Provided by the California Department of Education, Standardized Testing and Reporting Program. See *http://star.cde.ca.gov.*

plementary literacy program that claims to make up for 3,000 hours of pre-reading experiences that children need to become successful readers. In its first trial year, the program seems to have advanced four out of six children who otherwise might have needed the extra year of kindergarten.

In 1986 Ichinaga organized her parents in support of her methods when she fought and prevailed against a state ruling that required whole-language reading instruction in all California schools. The State Curriculum Commission rejected reading programs like hers that had a systematic phonics component, thus forbidding her use of state funds to purchase these text books. Six weeks after her parents papered the commission with protest letters, her texts were placed on the approval list.

Not even the building of the Century Freeway, which in 1992 forced Bennett to merge with the James Kew School, has stalled her school's achievement. Although Bennett-Kew now draws many of its students from a part of urban Inglewood fraught with drugs, violence, and crime, Ichinaga is no less committed to her students' success.

"We believe every child can learn," she says. "You've already lost if you begin making excuses, so our school culture is different. Here it's simple: If you have a complaint, give me a solution."

Bilingual education has also been a point of contention. Although 50 percent of her school is Hispanic and a full 30 percent have limited English proficiency, none is segregated to a bilingual program. Her school is allowed to do this because of an "achievement-based excuse" that Ichinaga gained from the State Department of Education. Yet, this waiver did not come easily.

In 1993 a state compliance team learned that Ichinaga's school was in violation of the state's bilingual mandates and threatened to withdraw the school's Title I funding. After three years of filing for exemptions, Ichinaga finally received a waiver based on her school's high test scores and the English fluency of her students. Without interruption, Tongan, Thai, and Spanish language students have been taught exclusively in English at Bennett-Kew and accelerated based on their individual abilities. California's recently passed Proposition 227 has lifted the bilingual constraint allowing the practice at Bennett-Kew to be the norm throughout the state.

For years Bennett-Kew students have also been district leaders in math. All students learn math concepts that are typically well above their grade level. This year the 3rd graders averaged in the 84th percentile on the Stanford-9.[18] All math instruction rigorously follows a monthly schedule that is enforced through regular unit tests. The results of these tests allow teachers to regroup and re-teach the students based on their individual mastery of the concepts.

Ichinaga believes that grade-level team teaching is one of the keys to success. In this way the teachers work together to improve each other's skills and master teachers are close at hand to refine a younger teacher's implementation of the curriculum. Referring to her explicit phonics and math curricula, Ichinaga says, "We want experts in Open Court, experts in Saxon math. We talk about the details of implementation all the time."

When a specific grade level is not working cohesively, Ichinaga personally works with the team and gives them extra time to put their program back on track. "Out of this forum, teacher leaders naturally arise," she notes. Already she has sent three of her teachers off to principalships in other schools and believes another three or four future principals are currently among her staff. Professional satisfaction is another clear benefit of her methods. Sixteen teachers now on staff either have children in the school or did in the past. Ichinaga even sent two of her grandchildren to the school. Two teachers and four aides are alumni. The average teacher tenure at Bennett-Kew is sixteen years.

In addition to the regular curriculum, in grades 2 through 5 a gifted and talented program offers certain students enrichment activities including: research projects, science presentations, art, poetry, music, dance, and leadership training. Ichinaga says, "We'd gladly put our top 25 percent against any in the country." But that's not the point. These elite students are successful because her mission is to secure the success of the entire school. "We believe that all students at every level can be successful in a common, comprehensive, academically oriented curriculum. We believe this irrespective of primary language or ethnic background."

And she puts her money where her mouth is. After the 1998 Stanford-9 results showed a falling off in 4th-grade reading, Ichinaga directed most of her discretionary funds into that class and personally pulled fifteen students for specialized instruction. In one year the 4th grade class average in both reading and math rose 14 percentile points.[19] "We believe all children can learn. And they do."

Notes:

18. Stanford-9 Achievement Test, Spring 1999. Provided by the California Department of Education, Standardized Testing and Reporting Program.
19. Stanford-9 Achievement Test, Spring 1999. These gains show a year over year improvement for the *grade level*; they do not reflect the gains achieved by a single set of students in a year's time.

Vanessa Beverly

Marcus Garvey School
2916 W. Slauson
Los Angeles, CA 90043
323.294.1154

Founded in 1975 by Anyim Palmer, Marcus Garvey is a private school with a strong Afro-centric curriculum that drives most students to score two years or more above grade level. In 1999, three 7th graders went on to attend West Los Angeles Junior College after they tested at the post-secondary level in all subjects.

"Our curriculum consists of the basic subjects: reading, writing, and spelling, for example, as well as more advanced material, especially in math and science," says Vanessa Beverly, now in her third year as the school's executive director. "But we try to attack each subject from its Afro-centric origin. In particular, we stress the African origins of math and science." At Garvey, most students do math that is advanced for their age: pre-schoolers add and subtract two-digit numbers; four-year-olds know their multiplication tables; 4th graders routinely study elementary algebra; students in the 9th and 10th grades often take calculus.

"Our children don't see enough African-Americans in textbooks and that tends to alienate them from school as a whole," Beverly explains. "We tell them that if their ancestors did it thousands of years ago, there is no reason why they can't do it today." In general, children are successful at Garvey because the curriculum encourages them to reset their personal expectations to a higher plane. All students study English, Spanish, and Swahili. The kindergartners are typically able to recite dialogues in both foreign languages.

Grades: PK-12
Students: 285
% Low-income: 75
Median Percentile in Reading: 80
Median Percentile in Math: 82[20]

School founder Palmer was a former high school administrator, public school teacher, and college professor who was frustrated by the public school system's abandonment of the inner-city black child. He

Notes:

20. Wide-Ranging Aptitude Test, Spring 1997. Provided by the Marcus Garvey School. The school no longer administers norm-referenced exams. This is the most recent date for which test data are available.

founded the school with $20,000 of his own money. "I guarantee you that any parent can do a better job teaching children than the public schools can," says Palmer. "If we can freely admit that public schools have not and will not truly educate our children, then it is important that we take our money and create our own institutions." Palmer is now a staunch supporter of school choice and competition in education.

"In a competitive environment, nobody would send their children to the schools we have today," says Palmer. "Why would I buy a bar of soap with no cleansing power? Similarly, why should I send my children to a school that only produces illiteracy? It's criminal that poor black children are forced to go to a failed school just because it's down the street."

Marcus Garvey is located in the Crenshaw district of south central Los Angeles. While most of its students hail from south central, some drive 30 or 40 miles each way to come to school. "Our children come from low-income or lower middle-income families who struggle to make education a priority," says Beverly. An education at Marcus Garvey costs $492 a month for the elementary grades and $508 for high school. Parents can also pay weekly or bi-weekly if that helps them meet the bills. This year the Children's Scholarship Fund sent 67 new children to the school.

Most parents of Garvey students, however, cannot afford to send their children to the school for a complete education. Instead, some just come for a year or two to get a foundation that their local schools have failed to provide. As a result, the school has to meet the needs of students with dramatically different levels of mastery at each grade level. Each class—but particularly the new children—is grouped into beginning, intermediate, and advanced sections. The object for the teachers at each grade level is to merge the three groups into one. With more children coming to the school in their later years, this challenge is becoming harder to meet. This year's 6th grade, for example, has new students who are non-readers as well as children reading at the high school and post-high school level.

Beverly, who was a teacher for 15 years in the school before becoming executive director, says the school is successful because of its teachers and that the teachers are successful because the school builds that capacity into them. "We don't want teachers with previous training," Palmer adds. "We want them trained in the Marcus Garvey method." The school has its own mandatory teacher training program that lasts about six months throughout the year. Palmer still teaches the African history component in this program so essential to the school's Afro-centric identity.

Both Beverly and Palmer stress that teachers at Garvey have to teach beyond their own skill set and often past their personal skill level. Motivation is the key to the method. Specialists, such as the math and science teacher who also teaches African history, rotate through the classrooms assisting the general classroom teachers. All throughout the year new teachers observe the master teachers to improve their in-class performance.

Marcus Garvey, for whom the school is named, was an American born in Jamaica who founded the Universal Negro Improvement Association, an organization that grew to over two million members at its height in the 1920s. Palmer says Garvey was a man who never gave up and who believed in his people. He was a worker, not an intellectual: he was a man who made things happen.

Garvey makes the perfect patron for this school, Palmer says, because through hard work and a dedication to improving the lives of blacks, his school faculty is making great things happen for their students. Now he wants to see two million more teachers like them.

Alfonso L. Jessie, Jr.

Cascade Elementary
2326 Venetian Drive, SW
Atlanta, GA 30311
404.752.0769

Cascade Elementary is a local public school that serves a 99-percent black population, 80 percent of whom come from low-income families. Although the school is located in the upscale middle-class neighborhood of Cascade Heights—a part of Atlanta famous for its powerful residents including senators, judges, college presidents, and even baseball great Hank Aaron—most of its students come from the local housing project not far from the school.

Regardless of where they come from, children at Cascade excel. In 1999, the 1st graders, for example, scored in the 92nd percentile in math and 98th in reading on the Iowa Test of Basic Skills. And the higher scores are not only in the lower grades. The 5th graders scored in the 82nd percentile in reading and 74th in math.[22] The year before, according to one study, Cascade ranked 7th out of the 1,064 elementary schools in all of Georgia.[23]

Cascade is a turnaround story. Only four years ago, before Alfonso Jessie came to Cascade from West Atlanta Elementary, the 5th graders were scoring in the 44th percentile in reading and 37th in math.[24] In just one year, Jessie had already turned around West Atlanta, but the surrounding area was too poor to keep the school open. Eventually, Jessie came to Cascade to replace Dubose Thomas, the school's principal who had suddenly died.

Grades: K-5
Students: 379
% Low-income: 80
Median Percentile in Reading: 74
Median Percentile in Math: 83[21]

"What we do is not rocket science," says Jessie, who has been in the school system now for 34 years. "In my school, our children are the only

Notes:

21. Iowa Test of Basic Skills, Spring 1999. Provided by Cascade Elementary.
22. *Ibid.*
23. *The 1998 Georgia Elementary Report Card for Parents*, Georgia Public Policy Foundation.
24. Iowa Test of Basic Skills, Spring 1996. *Georgia Public Education Report Card*. Provided by the Georgia Department of Education, Office of Research, Evaluation, and Testing. See *http://168.29.251.13.*

ones in the universe. We figure out what they need to know, and then we teach them until they have those skills." This is the three-part sequence of Jessie's formula for success: immediate personal attention, testing, and basic skills.

"Once a child knows you believe in him, he can compete anywhere in the world," says Jessie. "You have to get to know the child. You have to get to know the family. You have to spend some Saturdays with them. Then you can get to skill building." Jessie admits that this level of commitment can be daunting, but a few devices can cover a lot of ground in short order.

Cascade, for example, sends a contract home to parents obligating them to go over homework questions and to have their children in bed by 9 P.M. In this way children learn from their parents that school is a priority. In a similar vein, Jessie explains to parents at the beginning of the year that if their children misbehave in school, they will be personally escorted to their parents' place of work. Not surprisingly, Cascade has almost no discipline problems. To provide even further support, Jessie organized a corps of retired teachers, business owners, and other professionals from the area to visit the children in school and provide one-on-one tutoring. "School should be a place where positive role models abound," says Jessie. Every year he looks to expand this mentoring program.

A child's education at Cascade is tailored to his individual needs. At the beginning of the year, mornings are set aside for diagnostic testing until each student's portfolio of needs is determined. Throughout the year the children are then tracked by skill level and taught new material as they demonstrate mastery. The mastery of basic skills is the goal; regular assessment is the means.

"Children need constant encouragement," Jessie remarks, "[b]ut our encouragement has to be directed at learning." Cascade's regular testing regime provides the target objectives that the children need to inspire their increased performance. "We find every opportunity we can to say something positive, but we make sure that we are reinforcing their skill level by doing so."

"One problem in a large system is that decisions are made too far from the classroom," says Jessie. Cascade doesn't have this problem. Jessie trains his teachers himself and teaches several demonstration classes a day. "If I'm in the classroom, my teachers won't have any problems finding me or getting what they need," he points out.

Cynthia Collins

Marva Collins
Preparatory School
8035 S. Honore
Chicago, IL 60620
773.962.0101

The Marva Collins School was founded in 1975 as Westside Preparatory, a one-room school-house for ten students where, in the words of its founder, "No child would be allowed to fail." The school has recently moved to southside Chicago and has plans to expand to 500 students. With another school in Ohio, two in Wisconsin, and a teacher training program that has instructed more than a half million teachers, Marva Collins and her methods are a force to be reckoned with.

When asked what is the primary cause of student failure, without a moment's hesitation, Marva Collins replies: "Bad teachers. Teaching inabilities are as prevalent as learning disabilities."

Marva Collins tolerates no excuse for failure from her teachers, because she believes that the teacher alone limits a student's drive for excellence. "Any teacher can fail a student. But that's no sign of power. When a student fails, the teacher also fails. Teachers need to *believe* that every child can learn."

Teacher training forms the center of this school's daily life. Following Marva Collins' own personal commitment to lifelong learning, all of her teachers continually refine their craft in the classroom. Her daughter, Cynthia Collins, one of the original ten pupils at Westside Prep and now the headmistress of the school, heads up the school's ongoing staff development. Under her guidance, new teachers are assigned apprenticeships in the classrooms of master teachers who individually tutor them, both on the job and over the summer. In this way Collins maintains the continuity and integrity of her mother's no-nonsense, back-to-basics curriculum that is centered on phonics and memorization for the younger students, and higher-level reasoning and literary analysis for the older ones.

Grades: K-8
Students: 193
% Low-income: 70
Median Percentile in Reading: 51
Median Percentile in Math: 65[25]

Notes:

25. Iowa Test of Basic Skills, Spring 1999. Provided by Marva Collins Preparatory School.

"Teachers are a dime a dozen. Good teachers are rare," Cynthia Collins remarks. "We find dedicated individuals to embrace the methodology. Once they believe that all children can learn, it's only a matter of hard work."

And hard work it is. Neither the school day nor the school year is extended at Marva Collins, but every minute of class time is spent on task. Swiftly taken through one exercise after another, students are peppered with classical allusions at every turn and their teachers fully expect them to return the favor. Even among the youngest students, talk of Great Books fills the air. No matter what the subject or grade level, the children are expected to be persuasive in speech and equally effective on paper.

Like the ongoing teacher training that keeps the faculty sharp in the classroom, student performance is also regularly monitored and refined through weekly tests in all subjects every Friday. The older students maintain written journals, which promotes an interdisciplinary approach to their studies and provides a portfolio of their progress across subject areas. Regular research papers, beginning in the earliest grades, support the more routine exercises and provide a further outlet for articulate written expression.

Collins' teaching method, outlined in her latest book, *Marva Collins' Way*, is now promoted nationally by her son, Patrick, another of her original pupils and a former principal of the school.

Hellen DeBerry

Earhart Elementary
1710 East 93rd Street
Chicago, IL 60617
773.535.6416

Anyone who thinks that low-performing, under-funded, poorly equipped elementary schools can't be turned around has never met Hellen DeBerry. Over the course of her seven-year tenure as principal of Earhart Elementary in Calumet Heights, she made one of Chicago's desperately poor inner-city schools into the envy of the suburbs.

The Chicago public school system is, of course, still reeling from then-Secretary of Education William J. Bennett's claim that it was "the worst in the nation."[27] As recently as 1996, even though significant improvements have been made since Bennett's visit to the city, half of the children were working below grade level in nearly 80 percent of Chicago's schools.[28]

In the midst of this educational wasteland, Earhart proves what is possible. Between 1991 and 1998, the number of children in the entire school scoring at or above the national average soared 52 percentage points in reading and 46 points in math.[29] To take the 6th grade as but one example, during that same period, the class

Grades: PK-6
Students: 265
% Low-income: 82
Median Percentile in Reading: 70
Median Percentile in Math: 80[26]

Notes:

26. Iowa Test of Basic Skills, Spring 1998. Provided by the Department of Research, Assessment and Quality Reviews, Office of Accountability, Chicago Public Schools. See *http://webdata.cps.k12.il.us/*. These scores are for the last year that Hellen DeBerry was the principal of Earhart Elementary.
27. November 1987. See William J. Bennett, *The De-Valuing of America* (New York: Summit Books, 1992), p. 40.
28. Ron Wolk, "Strategies for Fixing Failing Public Schools," *Education Week*, November 4, 1998, p. 44.
29. The educational research organization Designs for Change has prepared a complete report on improved reading achievement in the Chicago public school system for a slightly different period. Of the 111 schools that substantially increased the number of children reading at or above the national norm between 1990 and 1997, Earhart Elementary topped the list. See Designs for Change, "What Makes These Schools Stand Out," October 1997, pp. 5-11.

national percentile ranking shot from 40th to 78th in reading and from 27th to 85th in math.[30]

Earhart Elementary is housed in a tiny, one-floor, tan brick building on the far southside of Chicago. Although the school may use a random lottery to draw up to 50 percent of its children from beyond the neighborhood, it is 99 percent black and 1 percent Hispanic. Eighty-two percent of the children qualify for the free and reduced lunch program.[31]

In 1991, the Board of Education slated Earhart for closure. With only 135 children enrolled, the school was so desperate for students that it advertised vacancies in the local post office and Pizza Hut. Earhart didn't even have its own principal; it was a branch of Hoyne Elementary, which administered the school from a half-mile away.

Under the Chicago School Reform Act of 1988, branch schools were to be newly organized with their own local school councils responsible for selecting their own school principals. Luckily, Earhart had an active and interested council eagerly looking to take advantage of this greater independence, and set out to find a principal who could establish an Afro-centric school with a concentration in math and science.

Hellen DeBerry, a former teacher, reading specialist, and assistant principal at Paderewski Elementary, got the job. When she arrived, there was no reading program in kindergarten and no significant writing anywhere in the curriculum; most of the learning was of a mundane skill-based sort that could never lead to the advanced curriculum in math and science that the council had envisioned. In response, DeBerry quickly educated her council on the school's specific needs and laid out a five-year plan to make Earhart the best school in Chicago.

First, she reestablished the school under the city's "options for knowledge" designation, which allows a school to draw from beyond its local neighborhood. Keeping the Afro-centric emphasis that the council wanted, DeBerry envisioned Earhart as a school for the humanities that would first address the language arts and then move on to improving its math, sciences, and social sciences until a full liberal arts curriculum

Notes:

30. Iowa Test of Basic Skills, Spring 1998. Provided by Board of Education of the City of Chicago.
31. Provided by Board of Education of the City of Chicago. Earhart's lottery does not significantly change the demographics of its student body, largely because the city's school system is one of the most segregated in the country. In the entire Chicago system of 569 schools, 90 percent of the children are minority and 84 percent are low-income. See Paul G. Vallas, "Saving Public Schools," Center for Educational Innovation, December 9, 1998, p. 1.

was in place. "The Afro-centric program was a means to an end. It wasn't the main focus," DeBerry notes. "Our mission was to provide every child with the well-rounded education necessary to make a responsible citizen." Reading became her top priority.

Her program concentrated not on reading methods, but on reading *comprehension*, and on developing classrooms that met the learning style of every student in the school. Phonics, memorization of sight-words, and literature-based approaches to reading were all brought together into a cohesive program that placed literacy at the center of school life.

DeBerry devoted an hour and a half each morning exclusively to reading. During this reading period, she canceled all physical education, music, art, and library hours so that the entire support staff could assist with the program. Committed to ongoing and universal staff development, DeBerry made sure that everyone in the school received sufficient training to teach the children how to read.

In line with DeBerry's vision to make Earhart a school for the humanities, this emphasis on reading developed a love of literature in the children. At Earhart, literature is emphasized in all subjects and provides a basis for an interdisciplinary approach to study so characteristic of excellent programs in the humanities. Grammar and basic essay composition lead quickly to higher-level research writing by the 2nd grade. Monthly oral presentations provide ample opportunities for public speaking. A Junior Great Books program, complete with literary seminars, gives the children a sophisticated forum for the development of their higher-order thinking skills and the art of conversation.

DeBerry believes that, given standards of excellence, children will always exceed your expectations of them. "All of our children are expected to work above grade level and to learn for the sake of learning," she says simply. "We instill a desire to overachieve. Give us an average child and we'll make him an overachiever." Last year's 6th grade was reading *To Kill a Mockingbird* while another class was writing its own stage play based on the story of the slave ship *Amistad*.

In an environment marked by failure and plagued by excuses protecting poor performance, DeBerry's commitment to excellence is unequivocal. "Economic status has nothing to do with intellectual ability," she declares flatly. "You have to set your standards regardless of constituency. Provide the free meals to those who need them, but keep your academic standards."

DeBerry invited parents to school, both to enlist their support and to show them what they can do to help their children succeed in school. But she says that it is not wise to depend on it: "You can't rely on parental involvement without it potentially becoming an excuse. Instead, we make the child responsible. Here, children learn there are consequences for their actions." The only alternative to this, DeBerry explains, is an instructional program weakened by a principal's attention to secondary matters. "We let our children understand that so many opportunities are available even if their parents can't or won't help. We talk a lot about the future, about good role models, and about careers. A school environment of achievement itself removes many obstacles."

Finding students is no longer a problem at Earhart; if anything, the school needs to find more space. The school has doubled in size since 1991 and has plans to expand to 8th grade later this year. Confident that the school was firmly rooted in a tradition of excellence and could stand on its own, DeBerry left the principal's office in 1998. She now works for the Chicago public school system as a troubleshooter helping to turn around other schools.[32] Earhart's new principal is Patricia Walsh.

Notes:

32. Hellen DeBerry can now be reached at 312.945.3811.

Craig Ergang

George Washington
Elementary
3611 East 114th Street
Chicago, IL 60617
773.535.5010

George Washington Elementary is a local public school on the east side of Chicago, not far away from Earhart Elementary. Although located in a neighborhood that houses immigrant families of Eastern European and Middle Eastern backgrounds, the area surrounding the school is predominantly Hispanic. Seventy-three percent of the children in the school today are Hispanic, most of whom come from hard-working blue collar Mexican and Puerto Rican families.

For a few years now Washington has enjoyed a growing reputation for excellence. From 1991 to 1997 Washington's school-wide reading scores improved more than any school in Chicago, except Earhart. In that same time period, the school's combined reading and math scores improved more than 85 percent of all Chicago schools.[34] Although these gains are relative to the past performance of many struggling schools, some of Washington's achievements can compete with any school in the land. This year's 3rd graders, for example, scored in the 92nd percentile on the Iowa Test of Basic Skills in math.[35]

Grades: PK-8
Students: 680
% Low-income: 76
Median Percentile in Reading: 58
Median Percentile in Math: 79[33]

"We have a good school," says Craig Ergang, now in his second year in the principal's office. "Families move into the neighborhood because they are attracted to the school and they know we don't select our students, as some magnet schools in the city are able to do."

Notes:

33. Iowa Test of Basic Skills, Spring 1999. Provided by the Department of Research, Assessment and Quality Reviews, Office of Accountability, Chicago Public Schools. See *http://webdata.cps.k12.il.us/*.
34. Designs for Change, "What Makes These Schools Stand Out," October 1997, p. 179.
35. Iowa Test of Basic Skills, Spring 1999. Provided by the Department of Research, Assessment and Quality Reviews, Office of Accountability, Chicago Public Schools.

But Ergang admits that the popularity of his school is a mixed blessing. Under the current funding formula, his projected school budget is based on the number of school-age children in the school's previous year attendance report, and not on the actual number of children in his building. Due to the shared housing arrangements common to this and many other low-income areas, Washington often has more students than were demographically projected. Families from outside the neighborhood also falsify their addresses to send their children to a better school. This year Washington will have nearly 100 more students than originally projected by the school system.

"With whatever we're given, we focus our time, money, and effort on the individual needs of the children," says Ergang. Of the school's $2.5 million budget, some $350,000 is supplemental money used entirely for improved instruction. In particular, this money pays for three instructional assistants who diagnose the needs of students for specialized tutoring. The rest of the money is used to pay for writing, art, and music teachers and to fund three positions in overcrowded classes.

Twenty-six years ago, Ergang left his career as a supervisor in the trust department at Continental Bank. After he had to fire several graduates of the Chicago public school system who couldn't function at a high school level, he decided to become a teacher and do something about it himself. He first came to Washington Elementary fourteen years ago as a reading resource trainer responsible for the in-house staff development of his fellow teachers. As a result of Ergang's influence, specialized instruction in reading and writing is now a hallmark of everyone's education at Washington.

"Reading and writing go together," Ergang remarks. "One of the surest ways to improve instruction across the board is to work on them as a whole." A dedicated language arts instructor teaches all students in grades 1 through 6 a specific course in narrative, persuasive, and expository writing. "Writing *as a process* is taught uniformly throughout the building," he continues. And because his students are well-instructed on how to write, they are freed up to focus more on content. "Despite our large percentage of second language students—Spanish, Urdu, and Serbo-Croatian are all represented—I have one of the best writing programs in the country," says Ergang. By way of proof, this school year 91 percent of 3rd graders met or exceeded state performance standards in writing. One hundred percent of 5th graders and 92 percent of 8th graders did the same.[36]

Ergang also spends his money on the arts. Washington has a very successful fine arts program for all grades, kindergarten through 8th, that, among others, has attracted the financial support of the Illinois Arts

Council. Even without such support, Ergang maintains that any successful school has to invest in the arts. "Art is the key to success for so many students," he remarks. "For low-income children it exposes them to so much they would never get elsewhere." The same is true of music. "There is a big correlation between musical proficiency and increased reading ability," he says. Students in grades 5 through 8 can play in the school band. Ergang pays his music teacher extra to assemble the band in the morning before school starts.

As far as staffing is concerned, Ergang says that a successful school attracts talented people who are willing to work hard to keep it that way. His teachers come early and stay late; the school's parents are equally loyal and hardworking.

A parent-run bilingual council is an especially important element of Washington's success. In Chicago, schools have three years to mainstream children into an all-English curriculum. Because Washington does not receive funding to maintain a child's second language throughout the school and because the parents want their children to be fluent in English, the bilingual council reinforces Ergang's insistence on English proficiency for all his students. "We prefer English as a Second Language over a pullout program in Spanish wherever possible," he notes, because it is the fastest and most effective way to make English the primary in-class language for everyone.

In the early grades, Washington emphasizes a traditional reading program of explicit phonics supported by a strong literature component. Almost every child at Washington is a reader by the end of kindergarten. "If you can read in Spanish, you can read in English," Ergang says forcefully. "Language acquisition leads to language transfer and we use that to our advantage when we can."

Notes:

36. Illinois Standards Achievement Test, September 1999. Provided by Washington Elementary.

James Coady

Morse Elementary
40 Granite Street
Cambridge, MA 02139
617.349.6575

Six years ago, so many students in Cambridge were drawn off to magnet schools in the Boston area that Morse was on the verge of closing. At the parents' request, James Coady introduced a comprehensive change to the curriculum installing Core Knowledge (see Appendix A) in all grades and at all levels.

"Our parents were convinced that a drastic solution was required if retaining the school was to be justified," Coady says of the decision to bring in the Core Knowledge Foundation and rework the school's curriculum. "We had a little difficulty in the beginning getting the staff on board—two teachers left—but that was a good thing in the end."

The parents at Morse were in fact instrumental in getting the new curriculum adopted. "Some at Central Administration [of Cambridge Public Schools] were adamantly opposed to Core Knowledge," Coady recalls. "They're influenced by the Harvard School of Education. They didn't want anything to do with a classical curriculum." The parents lobbied the local school board to approve their proposal. The superintendent supported the school's request. Until the bitter end, however, Coady says his superintendent was pressured by the local schools of education not to accept his school's wishes. And sometimes the attacks became personal. "I didn't realize that I was being called a racist for bringing Core Knowledge to the school," Coady remarks bluntly. "Some went so far as to call me a Nazi. But neither race nor poverty is the real issue here. Success is determined by a good curriculum and a good staff."

Grades: K-8
Students: 318
% Low-income: 65[37]
Median Percentile in Reading: 72
Median Percentile in Math: 84[38]

Morse is now the highest performing elementary school in Cambridge. Last year's 6th graders, for example, scored in the 71st percentile

Notes:

37. All of the schools included in the study have student populations that are 75 percent or more low-income. Morse is now reporting a low-income population significantly less than 75 percent. This reduction directly followed on the improved academic performance of the school.

38. California Achievement Test-5, Spring 1998. Provided by the Morse School.

in reading and 93rd in math. Eighty-five percent of the 8th graders passed the city-wide algebra exam in 1998, down from 92 percent the year before.[39] Although only 50 percent of the children at Morse officially sign up for the lunch program, nearly seven out of ten come from low-income families, many of whom are first-generation immigrants. Twenty-five percent of the children are Korean, 8 percent are Hispanic, and 27 percent are black.

Coady largely credits the school's success to Core Knowledge, a comprehensive, culturally integrated curriculum, that builds a child's knowledge step by step in all disciplines through all grades in a coordinated sequence. The curriculum maintains that this solid foundation of knowledge is both the necessary prerequisite and the natural springboard to more critical and creative thinking. Its opponents say that it is too rigid, doctrinaire, and Euro-centric.

"The curriculum guarantees that all our students receive a rich, varied, and cohesive course of studies," Coady replies. "It's hard to argue with our results."

Although the Core Knowledge Foundation was brought in to help with the transition to the new program, Coady says the curriculum is so specific that outside teacher training is hardly necessary. Implementing the program, he says, is very easy and is particularly well-suited for new teachers who might want more direction or who might find added comfort in the level of detail that it provides.[40]

Character education—specifically emphasizing the classical virtues—is another critical feature of the Morse curriculum. Using the *Core Virtues* resource guide published by the Link Institute, a non-profit Silicon Valley-based educational research organization, teachers at Morse plan a monthly, literature-based study of the virtues that is taught grade by grade in a three-year cycle.[41] In the first year, in the month of December, for example, each grade level incorporates the study of "generosity" into its preparations for the holiday season. The next year, "generosity" is refined to a reflection on "charity." And then, in the third year at the same time, the whole school focuses on "compassion." Like many other high-performing schools, Morse has found that the explicit study and discussion of character is central to the school's mission of shaping informed and responsible citizens.

Notes:

39. *School Improvement Plan 1999-2000*, Morse School for Cambridge Public Schools. Provided by the Morse School.
40. See *http://www.coreknowledge.org*.
41. See *http://www.linkinstitute.org*.

Coady strongly believes that regular testing is also critical. At Morse, teachers work in clusters and regularly share test results with their colleagues in order to drive achievement higher. Coady has found that using a carefully sequenced curriculum keyed to specific learning objectives such as Core Knowledge makes this kind of regular assessment that much easier. In April and May students prepare for the national exams. The results of mock tests are returned immediately and additional coursework is assigned where it is needed. A summer program is all but mandatory for students who require extra help.

"Those who need help get it, and get help that works," Coady says. "But it takes a hard-working staff." Homework sessions are held after school two days a week. Although they can leave at 2:45 P.M., many teachers are at the school from 7:30 in the morning to 5 at night.

Without a doubt, the new regime is working. Now students from the surrounding magnets are coming to Morse. Since Coady introduced the new program, the percentage of low-income students has dropped, demonstrating the economic stability that often comes with academic achievement. "When parents are given good choices, they take them," says Coady. "The higher-income families bring a lot to the school. Everyone benefits."

Ernestine Sanders

Cornerstone Schools
Association
6861 E. Nevada
Detroit, MI 48234
313.892.1860

Founded in 1991 in response to a challenge issued by Catholic archbishop Adam Cardinal Maida to provide better educational opportunities for the children of Detroit, the first of these "Christ-centered" schools was up and running less than a year after it was first conceived. Since then, Cornerstone has blossomed into a privately owned mini-school district of three elementary schools and one middle school providing outstanding education to some of Detroit's poorest children. With its rolling admissions policy, Cornerstone tries to accept all interested students regardless of skill level or special needs. The schools are nearly 100 percent black.

A Cornerstone education follows an academically rigorous, liberal arts curriculum deeply infused with character education to make what Ernestine Sanders, the president and CEO of the Cornerstone Schools Association, calls "an education where knowledge is centered in truth."

A clear record of achievement is in the making. Although the national percentile ranking of all four schools in math does not compare to their achievement in reading, this year's 8th graders scored in the 66th percentile. As for reading, Cornerstone's scores are especially impressive in the earliest years, with the kindergartners and the 1st graders scoring in the 82nd and 76th percentiles, respectively.[43]

Grades: PK-8
Students: 625
% Low-income: 75
Median Percentile in Reading: 65
Median Percentile in Math: 51[42]

To get these results, the schools emphasize real learning beginning with the youngest children. A pre-school program centered on phonics

Notes:

42. Stanford-9 Achievement Test, Spring 1998. Provided by the Cornerstone Schools Association. Although the school-wide test scores for 1999 do not meet the strict criteria for inclusion in this study, they are a strong indication of the school's continual improvement. The median percentile rankings in math and reading on the Stanford-9 Achievement Test for Spring 1999 were the 58th and 63rd percentiles, respectively.
43. Stanford-9 Achievement Test, Spring 1999. Provided by the Cornerstone Schools Association.

instruction and number awareness identifies the children with the greatest needs and provides them with the intensive instruction necessary to prepare them for success at Cornerstone.[44] Foreign language is studied every year at Cornerstone beginning in kindergarten.

Providing extra time in the classroom promotes Cornerstone's success.[45] An eleven-month school year extends to the second week in July. For students requiring still more help, or for parents with busy work schedules, supervised study hall is available every day from 7 to 8 in the morning and from 3 to 6 in the afternoon. Teachers are also provided with extra time each month to develop their lesson plans, attend workshops, and observe outside teaching methods.

Cornerstone emphasizes both the moral and academic development of the child. As Ernestine Sanders says, "At his core, a citizen is not a good citizen without virtue, without integrity, without honor, without a love for the other. Cornerstone in its humble way wants every child to leave us with what it takes to be a functioning member of our world." By design, a Cornerstone education works in concert with a child's family and community to make good American citizens.

The greatest hallmark of this outreach to the home is the signed "covenant" that each parent makes with the school. More than a written contract, the covenant is a bond that, as Sanders says, is "rooted in God's love for every person" and that commits each parent to cultivating the spiritual, social, and academic excellence of the child. At Cornerstone, the success of its students is the joint mission of the children, their parents, and the school working as one.

Cornerstone also demonstrates how old resources can be made new. One campus in Detroit, leased from the archdiocese, reinvigorated an unoccupied building on the site of the Sacred Heart seminary. Two others are housed in the former Lutheran School for the Deaf, a massive residential facility from a bygone era that is now completely renovated

Notes:

44. A trial pilot program before the start of 1997 reveals an achievement gap of between 20 and 30 points between students in the 1st grade who participated in the pre-school program and those who did not. Subsequent results show the continuing positive effect that pre-school has had on the later class work of the participating students. See *Cornerstone Schools 1997 Annual Report*, p. 14.

45. Cornerstone has been recognized for its effective use of time to help students meet high academic standards. See National Education Commission on Time and Learning, *Prisoners of Time: Schools and Programs Making Time Work for Students and Teachers* (Washington, D.C.: U.S. Government Printing Office, 1994).

and equipped to accept the latest computer technology. The fourth campus operates in the basement of a Lutheran church.

The conversion of old facilities is one thing, but the key to Cornerstone's success is its people. Sanders and the whole Cornerstone family have brought together hundreds of business, industry, and community leaders who have a vested interest in making sure the children at Cornerstone succeed. These "partners," as they are called, fund the school through "partnerships," each representing a $2,000 gift and a personal commitment to meet with the sponsored child four times a year. The goal is two partnerships per student. Over 500 partners are now in the program, with a 91-percent renewal rate year after year. Some have even sponsored a child's education from kindergarten to 8th grade and are now starting over again sponsoring a different child. Some have partnered with as many as ten children at once.

The financial gifts go a long way toward funding the school's mission, where the actual cost of an eleven-month Cornerstone education is $5,800 per student. Tuition is based on a "pay what you can" policy, with a full two-thirds of the school receiving some tuition assistance. The average tuition paid is $1,200; the maximum is $1,950. The lowest this year is $300. And even though this relatively modest amount is beyond the reach of many of the school's families, because the school seeks to nurture a culture of responsibility and ownership, everybody must pay something.

Between the partnership program and its tuition policy, Cornerstone aims to teach its parents, partners, and students alike that the greatest gift in life is to give of one's self to help another. In this way, Cornerstone's funding mechanism complements an idea both central to the school's educational philosophy and critical to its mission of urban renewal: Change must come from within. "The biggest thing in inner-city education is a transformation of attitude," Sanders explains. "Urban settings have low expectations, dilapidated buildings, and deflated children. Here we ask: What high expectations do you have for your own child? What are you willing to do to achieve those expectations? Cornerstone can help make them a reality."

The Cornerstone approach demonstrates to members of local communities that they are the real shareholders in the future of these school children. Their partnerships with the students raise the standard of achievement to a higher level. Sanders says, "When you partner with people of talent and knowledge you raise the level of expectations *and* the level of what you can give your children." Community partnerships at Cornerstone have led to the creation of a school agri-science garden project, an enhanced computer network, and an on-site health clinic, complete with a resident physician.

Although the school has expanded its own operation successfully, Sanders hesitates to say that she has developed a model that can be replicated elsewhere. "Cornerstone is not the answer to all things," she says. "We focus on helping those who come to us. If we can help others, we are certainly willing to try."

Patsy Burks

Owen Elementary
3033 15th Street
Detroit, MI 48216
313.596.7064

Testing, testing, and more testing is leading to phenomenal success at Owen Elementary. Teachers are grouped into testing teams so that all the stakeholders in the test results have a say in the test preparations. The 4th grade teacher responsible for next year's students, for example, actively works with the 3rd grade teacher preparing those children for their end-of-the-year exam. This team approach delivers extraordinary results.

In 1999, 94 percent of Owen 4th graders passed the state math exam compared with 49 percent of all 4th graders in Detroit.[47] Eighty percent passed the reading exam.[48] The school-wide results on the Metropolitan-7 are even more impressive for a curriculum that is driven by the performance measures of a state exam. Last year's 5th graders, for example, posted a mean score at the 98th percentile in reading and 90th in math.[49] The 1st and 3rd grades also had mean scores in both math and reading above the 85th percentile.[50]

Grades: PK-5
Students: 457
% Low-income: 82
Median Percentile in Reading: 80
Median Percentile in Math: 79[46]

"Some call this teaching to the test," says Patsy Burks, the school's principal for the past twelve years, "But the state exam prescribes what the children need to know and we adjust our annual calendar to meet those expectations."

As Burks explains it, Detroit Public Schools mandates her curriculum based on the State of Michigan's *Benchmarks, Goals, and Objectives*. Although this framework is fairly rigid, each school may adapt and modify its curriculum to meet the needs of its students. Owen does not

Notes:

46. Metropolitan Achievement Test-7, Spring 1999. Provided by Owen Elementary.
47. Michigan Educational Assessment Program, 1999. Provided by the Michigan Department of Education.
48. *Ibid.*
49. Metropolitan Achievement Test-7, Spring 1999. Provided by Owen Elementary.
50. *Ibid.*

alter its curriculum, but instead focuses its attention on expert teaching practices. According to Burks, a simple motivator makes this kind of teaching possible. "People ask us: How do you do it?" Burks remarks. "You have to see it for yourself. Our teachers like teaching. Our teachers are happy here. A happy teacher can be a powerful force."

In a similar vein, Burks is particularly proud of Owen's carefully cultivated home-like environment, which has a positive effect on teachers and students alike. "We want a warm and loving environment to help *raise* the standards, not to lower them," says Burks. "In order to be effective you have to make your school attractive. Our school is an oasis. The children learn well because they want to be here."

While so many high-income schools count on a child's well-ordered life at home to supplement his learning in school, Owen's focus on a nurturing setting is designed to support the high expectations of the classroom. "Our children come to school facing a lot of challenges. But it's our job to make those challenges bring out their best. With the right support and incentives in place a challenge can become a source of strength and pride, rather than just a barrier to overcome," Burks explains. "We teach the children that being smart is something earned through hard work. We don't ask the children 'How bad off are you?' We say, 'Find out how good you can be.'"

The whole staff works together to create an environment that Burks says is non-threatening to the parents, however demanding it is of the students. "We encourage parental involvement in less formal ways," she says. School can be intimidating to some parents and so Burks and her staff make an effort to relieve that pressure by providing helpful services they might not receive elsewhere. The school circulates voter registration cards at election time, for example, and sometimes the parents receive the free lunch. "In this way we get to know them better, we get to know their children better, and they get some much needed help without the threat of social services coming into their home," Burks says. In this way Owen becomes more of a home for its students, more of an institution that its parents will turn to, and a more effective school as a result.

Ronald Williams

Newberry Elementary
4045 29th Street
Detroit, MI 48210
313.596.4966

In 1998 four Detroit children were killed in a fire at their grandmother's house while their mother was in the hospital giving birth to her sixth baby. Two of the children lost in the fire were Newberry students. The school was often cited in news reports as the glue that held this fragile community together.

A beautiful middle-class neighborhood in the late '60s, Newberry is now an extremely poor part of southwest Detroit on the far edge of the city's empowerment zone. Most of the parents who send their children to Newberry don't work. There are no stores of any kind for miles. The school is set among the vast, vacant lots and abandoned houses left in the wake of Detroit's white flight to the suburbs.

In this bleak landscape, Newberry Elementary shines like a beacon of

> Grades: PK-5
> Students: 610
> % Low-income: 90
> Median Percentile in Reading: 66
> Median Percentile in Math: 68[51]

hope. In March 1998, the 4th grade class scored in the 80th percentile in reading and in the 82nd in math on the Metropolitan-7. Weaker scores in the 2nd and 3rd grades pulled down the school-wide median, but the 1st graders scored in the 81st percentile in reading and in the 77th in math.[52]

"Our success follows on a single principle," Williams says. "If a child can't learn the way I teach, then I must learn to teach the way she learns."

All teachers at Newberry work in grade-level clusters and share performance results and teaching tips with each other in order to accelerate student performance across disciplines. After last year's disappointing test scores came in, for example, the 2nd grade teachers physically reorganized the entire building to facilitate better communication among all grade-level teachers.

Notes:

51. Metropolitan Achievement Test-7, Spring 1998. Provided by Newberry Elementary.
52. *Ibid.*

"I give my teachers whatever they need to get the job done and then hold them accountable for the results," Williams says. "Administrators need to unleash their teachers' talent. If you convince everyone in the staff to create a can-do atmosphere, it's only a short step from figuring out *how* to get it done. But once you allow excuses in, it isn't long before your teachers aim for nothing more than just fewer hassles."

Four days a week for two hours a day Newberry teachers run a voluntary after-school program in reading and math. The results are stunning. In 1999, 77 percent of the 5th graders passed the state writing exam; the year before 91 percent passed. In 1999, 90 percent of the 4th graders passed the state math exam.[53] For those who require even more help, Newberry hosts a Summer Learning Academy.

Newberry is a disciplined school. But, as science teacher Walter Smith points out, class discipline does not come easily for its students and teachers: "Education begins and ends with the family. In order to educate an unsteady child, we first have to overcome a crisis in the home. For some that's an excuse. Here there's no excuse making, but as teachers we have to know that we are also doing the work of parents." Smith comes to school by 7:20 each morning to give himself almost an hour and a half to prepare for the day. He spends his afternoons supervising voluntary lab projects. "We don't just keep them busy," says Smith. "We're giving them an opportunity."

This kind of dedication pays off. In 1998, 83 percent of the 5th graders at Newberry passed the state science exam in a state where 40 percent passing is the norm.[54]

Notes:

53. Michigan Educational Assessment Program, 1999. Provided by the Michigan Department of Education.
54. Michigan Educational Assessment Program, 1998. Provided by the Michigan Department of Education.

Alyson Barillari

Fourteenth Avenue School
186 Fourteenth Avenue
Newark, NJ 07103
973.733.6940

Operated for years as a regular local public elementary and middle school (K-8), Fourteenth Avenue began serving handicapped children bused-in from all over the city once the neighborhood deteriorated and the local population declined. Fourteenth Avenue is now a balanced regular and special education elementary school (K-4) that serves the broadest range of disabilities.

This year, of the 210 children in the school, 76 are special education students spread out over nine classes, both self-contained and mainstreamed with regular education students. The self-contained classes are reserved for children who are multiply handicapped, pervasively disturbed, or mentally retarded.[56] Otherwise, children with special needs share resource teachers in classrooms alongside their peers in the regular educational program. The end result is that every student at Fourteenth Avenue benefits from the resources and the expertise made available through the special education program. The school has strict academic growth standards for all children regardless of disability, regardless of family background. Ninety-nine percent of the students are black. Ninety-eight percent come from low-income families.

Although it is more difficult to quantify succinctly the academic achievement of the special education students, the results in the regular education program are phenomenal.

Grades: K-4
Students: 210
% Low-income: 98
Median Percentile in Reading: 90
Median Percentile in Math: 95[55]

Notes:

55. Stanford-9 Achievement Test, Spring 1998. Provided by Fourteenth Avenue School. These results reflect the regular education scores for grades 2 and 3. No special education students are included.
56. Fourteenth Avenue serves children of all needs including: the neurologically impaired and those with traumatic brain injury; the emotionally disturbed; the trainable mentally retarded; and the autistic. Wherever possible, Fourteenth Avenue tries to include these children in at least some of the activities of the regular education students.

For the past several years the regular education students have posted mean scores above the 90th percentile on the Stanford-9 achievement test. In 1998, the 2nd grade had a mean score in the 94th percentile for both reading and math, while the 3rd graders came in at the 86th and 95th percentiles, respectively. For accountability purposes, the 4th grade is assessed using the state-mandated elementary proficiency assessment (ESPA), which is not a norm-referenced exam. In 1999, of the 51 schools in the district with 4th graders, Fourteenth Avenue was first in math and ninth in language arts. The special education students at Fourteenth Avenue are only required to take the Stanford Diagnostic test, but all are expected to demonstrate regular academic gains on their functioning levels from year to year.

It is the school's emphasis on testing and assessment that fosters its culture of excellence. "We work backwards," says Barillari. "Based on the Core Curriculum Content Standards expected at each grade level, we work in class accordingly. From kindergarten—from day one—we tell them what tests they are taking this year and what tests they will take next." When children don't perform well, Barillari looks carefully at the results and the *teaching* that caused it. "Is there a pattern to the assessment? Did they do poorly in all areas or only in some?" she asks. "You then identify the teacher with the best results and get *that teacher* to teach the others."

Barillari is quick to note that such a system, when well managed, will not intimidate the staff, but only encourage further achievement. "You have to find everyone's strengths and weaknesses. Everyone will have something to add. We concentrate on assessment so much that it becomes a reward mechanism. We use it as a vehicle to prove how good we are."

Master teaching is what sets Fourteenth Avenue apart. "No one needs to leave the building for staff development," Barillari continues. "I have a staff of veterans who teach each other." For example, four years ago Barillari found a parochial school teacher at the Newark job fair who clearly had skills that could benefit the entire staff. Now that teacher runs a math lab at all grade levels in tandem with the developmental teachers who team-teach every day alongside the regular classroom teachers. This arrangement not only brings continuity to the math program, but it also builds added teaching expertise into the faculty and allows the developmental teachers to focus on content. Whereas in many schools the regular classroom teacher is unqualified to teach certain disciplines and is only further distracted by the needs of certain students, at Fourteenth Avenue all the teaching resources available are concentrated on raising the academic proficiency of all students in all subject areas.

Irwin Kurz

P.S. 161—
The Crown School
330 Crown Street
Brooklyn, NY 11225
718.756.3100

When principal Irwin Kurz first came to Crown thirteen years ago, its scores sat in the bottom quartile of District 17 in Brooklyn. Now they proudly stand as the best in the district and rank 40th out 674 elementary schools in all of New York City.[58]

Although they have to pack their students 35 to a classroom, the teachers at Crown make neither class size nor anything else an excuse for poor performance. Kurz says, "It's a lot of garbage that poor kids can't succeed." Nearly every child at Crown qualifies for the free or reduced-price lunch.

Set in Crown Heights, an area of Brooklyn rightly proud of its Caribbean influences, but working hard to overcome the turmoil of its recent riots, the Crown School is a neighborhood public school serving poor minority children. Ninety-one percent of its students are black; 8 percent are Hispanic.

From the outside you could never tell that you were looking at one of the best schools around.Inside its doors the signs of accomplishment are everywhere. In stark contrast to the world around it, Crown is a study in success that promotes achievement at every turn. Every square inch of hallway groans under the weight of student projects, presentations, book reports, and the certificates of excellence they have received. "The physical plant has to show the kids that you care about them," Kurz remarks. The

Grades: K-8
Students: 1,342
% Low-income: 98
Median Percentile in Reading: 71
Median Percentile in Math: 78[57]

sparkling corridors shimmer with waxed floor reflections of the lights overhead and the awards that line the walls.

Crown is a shamelessly proud institution that looks and feels like a private school from the moment you cross the threshold. Even the

Notes:

57. California Test of Basic Skills and California Achievement Test-5, Spring 1998. Provided by P.S. 161 for grades 3-8.
58. April 1999. Provided by the New York City Board of Education, Division of Assessment and Accountability, Test Analysis Unit.

plaid-uniformed students sport navy sweaters with an ornate Crown insignia emblazoned on the chest. "It's pretentious, but I want it that way," Kurz says with a wry smile. "We're trying to make a very special school for these children."

The school is clearly the product of Kurz design. Its order, efficiency, and calm self-assurance are all a reflection of the man who put them in place. Yet Kurz maintains that nothing at Crown is unobtainable elsewhere. "High expectations aren't enough," he says. "You have to *intend* on actually getting the job done. If you really intend on doing it, it will happen." When Kurz instituted the school uniforms, for example, he simply sent out a letter notifying the parents where to pick them up.

Kurz gets to work by 6:15 each morning and is able to eliminate many of that day's problems before anyone else even knows they exist. "It's the easiest way to build morale in a school," he says. "If you solve the little problems, they'll trust you with the big picture."

As a reflection of this thinking, Kurz makes sure that success comes early and often to his students. Children who don't succeed in the earliest years are quick to believe that they are ill-equipped for school. In response, Kurz established literacy in kindergarten as a hallmark of his program. "If we let them, children will attribute any failure in school to a lack of natural ability," Kurz says. "Here we teach them that hard work creates ability." More than 80 percent of Crown's kindergartners can read.

Blouke Carus, former president of Open Court Publishing, says Crown is the best Open Court school in the country. Much more than the school's implementation of the Open Court phonics curriculum makes this so. Irwin Kurz has figured out how to develop the reading habit.

Classrooms literally overflow with books. Kindergartners who can read and older students who write five book reports each year are awarded a certificate that is hung on the wall and a button they can wear on their uniform. They are the members of the Principal's Reading Club. A monthly newspaper of student book reviews called *By-Lines* keeps the school abuzz with book talk. A weekly book sale is the center of school life. Over 2,600 books were sold in the two days before Christmas— with thousands more sold throughout the year. All books are sold, at a loss, for $1 each—fund-raisers cover the balance. Student advertising executives and inventory clerks earn bookstore pay to buy their own books in exchange for their work promoting and running the store. The bookstore is a tabletop.

In 1996 Kurz added a selective middle school called the Crown School of Law and Journalism.[59] Now the 6th grade at Crown has the second highest reading scores in all of New York State.[60] Taken together, the 6th, 7th, and 8th grades in 1998 scored in the 93rd percentile in reading and in the 96th in math.[61] In 1998, the entire 8th grade passed the New York State algebra Regents exam—84 percent with distinction.[62]

As Kurz is quick to explain, success at Crown is primarily the work of a well-integrated staff. In all grade levels children are assigned to a single teacher for all instruction, but the improvement of instruction is a collective responsibility shared by the entire faculty. Kurz instituted a system of peer evaluation where teachers on the same grade level observe each other solely to improve each other's teaching. The sense of professionalism among the staff is palpable.

Kurz is himself a teacher turned principal, who understands that teachers must be free to adapt their styles to the needs of their students. He believes that only the individual teacher knows what is best for her classroom and that real teacher autonomy and respect for individual teaching style are necessary to bring it out. The wide variety in classroom layout, decoration, and design shows a vibrant practice at work. But it is Kurz's job to supply his teachers with whatever they need to improve their instruction, even if that means finding funds for outside seminars or additional supplies. This commitment to his teachers makes for low teacher turnover: The average tenure at the school is fifteen years.

In exchange, Kurz expects results. Testing is the key to Crown's internal assessment. Mock tests in reading and mathematics are administered in December, January, and March. Teachers receive the results immediately and then tutor the children based on an exact portfolio of individual needs. Within two or three days students requiring remediation are assigned to one of the 26 paraprofessional tutors on staff. Kurz is the test hawk behind this data-driven approach. "You have to set clear and mea-

Notes:

59. Grades PK-5 at Crown average 215 students each. The Crown School of Law and Journalism accepts the best applicants from the same neighborhood: grades 6-8 average 55 students each.
60. Randal C. Archibold, "The Top Schools," *The New York Times*, April 11, 1999, sec. 1, p. 34. See *Separate and Unequal: The Reading Gap in New York's Elementary Schools*. The Public Policy Institute of New York State, p. 44.
61. California Test of Basic Skills and California Achievement Test-5, Spring 1998. Provided by the New York City Board of Education, Division of Assessment and Accountability.
62. *New York City Board of Education 1997-1998 Annual School Report*, "P.S. 161 - The Crown School," p. 6. See http://207.127.202.63.

surable objectives for everyone," Kurz notes. "I don't know what other people use. We use tests." Of the 100 students who received tutoring after one such recent mock test—50 children in reading and 50 in math—99 passed when test day came around.

With genuine humility, Kurz says his job doesn't amount to much: he might set the goal, but it is for the others to reach it. He says quite frankly, "My teachers do all the work."[63]

Notes:

63. In September 1999, Kurz was made the Brooklyn Regional Instructional Superintendent for the Chancellor's District. The Chancellor's District (District 85) is comprised of schools in Brooklyn, Manhattan, Queens, and the Bronx that grossly underperformed on the state and city assessments in reading and math. Kurz is now directly responsible for the 15 District 85 schools located in Brooklyn. He can be reached at M.S. 391 on 718.221.0701.

Mary Kojes

P.S. 122—The Mamie
Fay School
21-21 Ditmars Boulevard
Long Island City, NY 11105
718.721.6410

P.S. 122 is a local public school in Queens that also houses a district-wide gifted and talented program in grades 6-8. Starting this year, a strand of students in grades 1 through 5 will participate in a Core Knowledge magnet program that will draw its students from all 25 schools in District 30. The idea is to let the magnet and gifted programs set the pace for the whole school.

Reflecting the population of its surrounding neighborhood, the school is 32 percent Hispanic; 21 percent Asian, Indian, or Pacific Islander; and 10 percent black. The remaining population of whites is largely made up of immigrant children of Greek, Italian, and Eastern European descent. More than seven out of ten children at P.S. 122 come from low-income families, but neither family background nor primary language is a barrier to achievement at this school.

Overall, P.S. 122 ranks 38th in math and 48th in reading out of more than 1,000 elementary and middle schools in New York City. Last year's 3rd graders scored in the 80th percentile in math and the 68th percentile in reading. The middle school results are even more impressive. The 6th graders had mean scores in the 96th percentile in math and 93rd in reading.[65] One hundred percent of all three 6th grade classes tested at the highest level in reading on the California Test of Basic Skills—the highest reading scores in all of New York State.[66]

"This is like a Title I school, only we don't get Title I funding," says principal Mary Kojes, referring to the federal formula grant program. Kojes, now in her third year as principal, adds, "Some parents don't fill out the forms for the free lunch because of language problems or out of embar-

Grades: K-8
Students: 1,230
% Low-income: 73
Median Percentile in Reading: 77
Median Percentile in Math: 82[64]

Notes:

64. California Test of Basic Skills and California Achievement Test-5, Spring 1999. Provided by the New York City Board of Education, Division of Assessment and Accountability.
65. *Ibid.*
66. Randal C. Archibold, "The Top Schools," *The New York Times*, April 11, 1999, sec. 1, p. 34.

rassment." Although only 20 percent of the students are officially classi-
fied as having limited English proficiency, more than 40 percent come
from homes where English is the second language. Mary Kojes is herself
a first-generation immigrant who came to America from Greece when
she was five years old. While many schools with fewer new immigrants
blame poor reading scores on their second-language students, Kojes sees
a unique opportunity for excellence.

"Foreign children can push the academics upward," she says. "Immigrant children and their parents are looking to make a better life and
they know that education is the way to move up. In our school they
bring the others with them." During a tour of the school, a small 4th
grade girl in traditional Indian garb reads aloud a fable for discussion
with her classmates. "Many of us don't take advantage of what's here
unless we learn from others that this opportunity isn't available the
world over," Kojes adds.

Ninety-five percent of all students who graduate from P.S. 122 go to
Townsend, Bronx Science, Stuyvesant, or Brooklyn Tech: four of the
highest-ranking high schools in New York and among the very best in
the country. However, only a third of all the students who come to P.S.
122 for elementary school eventually graduate, because grades 6
through 8 represent a more selective program.

A former assistant principal of ten years, a district staff developer, and
math instructor, Kojes came to P.S. 122 with a plan to build on its success and increase the academic rigor of all grades and in all subjects.
"This is a very traditional school," Kojes remarks. "My predecessor was
the principal here for 23 years and gave the school a strong foundation."
With the basic skills in place, Kojes figured the school was ready for the
next step.

Kojes's goal is to get P.S. 122 among the top ten in the city. "I want a
school-wide average in the 90s in math and in the 80s in reading," she
says flatly. "My focus is on our regular school. That's where we can
make the biggest difference. The children in grades 6 through 8 will
make it no matter what. Our assignment now is to learn from their success and drive the achievement of the whole school upwards."

"You can't make a difference as an autocrat and you can't do it alone,"
she adds. "You have to do it in steps and as a team." Like so many other
high-performing principals, she made reading the priority and she made
sure that the curriculum clearly defined what should be taught at each
grade level.

"Not all teachers are created equal," Kojes says candidly. Kojes pairs
her new teachers with more experienced teachers to learn how they
manage a classroom, work with parents, and shape daily lessons from

the defined curriculum. The end result of this ongoing staff development is improved teaching.

"The curriculum states the objectives," Kojes explains. "But an objective has to be turned into an aim that speaks to a very specific skill." This is what her teachers teach each other to do. There are any number of ways to teach any one skill, but the skills themselves are very specific and have to be developed in a specific sequence. More than anything else this fact has merited Kojes's increased respect for the Core Knowledge curriculum and the need for clear assessment.

"You can't do your own thing in the classroom and then expect a child to return anything valuable," Kojes remarks. "If children do well on *your* tests and bomb out on the national exams there is something wrong with what you're teaching. But if you're testing all along and assessing them according to the standards for that grade you should not be surprised at the end of the year during the final exam."

Gregory Hodge

Frederick Douglass
Academy
2581 Adam Clayton
Powell, Jr., Blvd.
New York, NY 10039
212.491.4107

Maverick school principal Lorraine Monroe established the Frederick Douglass Academy in 1991 on the site of a failed middle school in central Harlem to prove that low-income, inner-city minority children could match any standard of achievement in the land.[67] She was right.

Within a few years of FDA's founding, its high school Regents scores in English, U.S. history, and pre-calculus rivaled those of New York exam school powerhouses Stuyvesant and Bronx Science. In 1998, 93 percent of FDA students who took the U.S. History Regents passed, compared with 58 percent across the city. Similar scores were made in English and pre-calculus with passing rates of 88 percent and 87 percent, respectively. In the Global History Regents–a two-year survey course of world civilizations considered by many the most challenging New York State exam–95 percent of 166 FDA students passed, compared with the citywide average of 54 percent.[69]

Even after a slight decline the year before, in 1998 the middle school test scores ranked 12th out of 235 in New York City, 32 percentage points higher than the city average in reading and 26 points higher in math.[70]

Grades: 7-12
Students: 1,030
% Low-Income: 80
Median Percentile in Reading: 73
Median Percentile in Math: 81[68]

Gregory Hodge took over from Lorraine Monroe in 1996 and is committed to extending Monroe's vision of educational opportunity. His

Notes:

67. See Lorraine Monroe, *Nothing's Impossible: Leadership Lessons from Inside and Outside the Classroom*. New York: Public Affairs, 1997.
68. California Test of Basic Skills and California Achievement Test-5, Spring 1998, for grades 7-8 only. Grades 9-12 at FDA take the New York Regents, which are not nationally normed. Provided by New York City Board of Education, Division of Assessment and Accountability.
69. *Overview of Examination Results and Related Statistics for the 1997-1998 School Year*, "Frederick Douglass Academy." Provided by Office of Educational Technology of the Office of the Chief Executive for School Programs and Support Services.

goal is a full scholarship to college for every graduate. College preparation at FDA now begins in the 7th grade. A required program in test preparation, post-secondary research writing, and college counseling keeps the children focused on their collegiate future. Students are even required to make a certain number of college visits each year, again, beginning in the 7th grade.

The program is working. The school will graduate its largest class of 123 students this year, sending them to Yale, Princeton, Cornell, Dartmouth, Duke, Tufts, Amherst, and the best of the traditionally black colleges, including Morehouse, Lincoln, Morris Brown, and Xavier.

The intersection of 149th Street and 7th Avenue used to be a proud center of black America. Stylishly dressed professionals strolled the boulevard on their way to the in-vogue theaters that produced the jazz greats of the be-bop era and the poetry of the Harlem Renaissance. Langston Hughes was a teacher here. Now the embattled bunker of a school squats above the noise of the Lenox terminal subway station with only the grime of a full-service car wash across the street to keep it company. Yet, amid this scene, pride is alive in Harlem.

In a hurry to get to class on time, the students pour through the front doors of the Academy, inspecting their uniforms in the lobby mirrors as they pass by. Hodge pulls a few aside to say hello and then sends them off as they pass muster. Overhead, they are greeted by a mural of Frederick Douglass and a single line from the self-educated slave turned abolitionist: "Without struggle, there is no progress."

"That's what we're about," says Hodge. "Without an education these children are slaves to the world they live in. With real learning, there's no end to what they might do."

Frederick Douglass is a local public school of choice that draws 80 percent of its students from Harlem's District 5, with the rest accepted on the basis of an interview and two written recommendations. A reflection of the local neighborhood, the student body is 79 percent black, 20 percent Hispanic, and 1 percent Asian or white.[71] Hodge makes an

Notes:

70. Provided by Frederick Douglass Academy based on New York Board of Regents report on the Manhattan Superintendency for 1997-1998. Eighty-two percent of the middle school were above passing in reading compared to the citywide average of 49.6 percent passing; 88.9 percent of the middle school were above passing in math compared with the citywide average of 63.1 percent passing.

71. *Overview of Statistics and Performance Results for the 1997-1998 School Year,* "Frederick Douglass Academy." Provided by Office of Educational Technology of the Office of the Chief Executive for School Programs and Support Services.

effort to open his doors to all students, but you have to *choose* FDA. "If you're not interested in hard work, then FDA's not for you," Hodge remarks candidly. "It's pretty self-selecting."

To establish the disciplined and orderly environment that characterizes FDA, Monroe drew up the school's now-famous "12 non-negotiables" and insisted on a school uniform. Ranging from the banal ("gum chewing and candy are prohibited") to the hortatory ("learn to disagree without being disagreeable"), the non-negotiables clearly dictate that school is a place where respect for one's self, one's associates, and everyone's property is a prerequisite for academic success. Parents agree to enforce their child's commitment both to the non-negotiables and to the rigors of a college preparatory education. The school is permitted to dismiss students who fail to comply. As for the uniforms, Monroe has said memorably that they get "the children to focus on what's in their heads, not on their backs."[72]

Like his predecessor Monroe, Hodge believes that discipline emerges from a clearly defined school culture focused on academics. He has recently introduced a student creed based on one from Morehouse College. According to this creed, "The community of scholars at FDA is dedicated to personal and academic excellence." The students call this school-wide commitment to excellence and exemplary behavior "being Academy." As Hodge says, "The world around them openly rejects their commitment to excellence. That's why we expect them to be Academy twenty-four hours a day, seven days a week. No exceptions."

Hodge wants to set his students up for success. If he had the funding, he would keep the school open from 6:30 A.M. to 10:00 P.M. every day. "By giving students a safe place you may be able to increase performance. We do everything we can to help, but we place the burden on them to get the job done," Hodge says. For now, the school is open from 7:30 A.M. to 8 P.M. weekdays and from 9 A.M. to 4 P.M. on Saturdays for SAT preparation, AP calculus, AP physics, AP English, and other academic subjects.

Despite extraordinarily limited resources, no activity goes wanting at FDA. A mandatory year of music theory and technique for every child in the school yields a string orchestra, a pop ensemble, and a variety of jazz combos. The school also fields nineteen sports teams including a fencing club.

Notes:

72. Dana Parnell, "From a Brokendown School to a Prestigious Harlem Academy," *Manufacturer's Association of Northwest Pennsylvania Business Report*, November 1997, p. 7.

According to Hodge, you won't get improved performance unless you expect the highest level of performance across the board: "You have to demand more of your students while providing them with the structure to meet those demands. The more difficult the curriculum, the greater the likelihood your students will be successful." He insists upon the same high standards for his teachers.

Among a population of students the education establishment would earmark for failure, Hodge speaks only of success. He demands that everyone on his staff do the same. "Everyone—students, teachers, parents, and the surrounding community—all believe that FDA can produce scholars," he says, "and we have." Teachers have to buy into the school culture that Hodge has created or they won't last long. "The whole school is focused on college. Every student is going to college. Every teacher is teaching a future college graduate. If you don't believe that, then I don't believe you're welcome here."

David Levin

KIPP Academy
250 East 156, Room 418
Bronx, NY 10451
718.665.3555

After working with Michael Feinberg to found the Knowledge Is Power Program (KIPP) in Houston, David Levin successfully transplanted the innovative educational formula to the South Bronx. The former Teach for America teacher founded KIPP in New York in 1995. The school is now the highest performing middle school program in the five districts that comprise the Bronx. A neighborhood school that is 45 percent black and 55 percent Hispanic, KIPP is housed in the same building and draws from the same population as I.S. 151, the lowest-performing school in the district.

If you go looking for KIPP Academy you'll have a hard time finding it. No signs anywhere announce its whereabouts except the signature banner "There are no shortcuts!" that hangs outside the fourth floor wing that the school shares with a citywide special education program. Confounding matters still more, KIPP's test scores are kept aggregated with even another school, P.S. 156, making it impossible to find through the official channels. "This arrangement is what allows us to exist," Levin concedes. "Call it a price on our independence." And a heavy price it is—KIPP only receives money from the Board of Education for faculty salaries; the rest of its funding Levin has to raise independently.

Grades: 5-8
Students: 223
% Low-income: 95
Median Percentile in Reading: 69
Median Percentile in Math: 81[73]

Even with these constraints on Levin's program, the school's record of achievement is astounding. The average reading score for students who have gone to KIPP for two years is in the 64th percentile. After three years that average skyrockets to the 78th percentile.[74] As for math, in

Notes:

73. California Test of Basic Skills and California Achievement Test-5, Spring 1998. Provided by KIPP Academy.
74. These multi-year results are provided by KIPP Academy based on the California Test of Basic Skills administered by the New York City Board of Education from 1996-1998. These gains cannot be easily verified by the New York City Board of Education because 5th grade KIPP results are not disaggregated from the test scores of P.S. 156.

1998 the 6th and 7th graders ranked in the 81st and 85th percentiles, respectively.[75]

Because KIPP operates in the midst of another school almost hostile to its rigors and discipline, daily life brings about some unusual juxtapositions. At lunch on any given day, children from the same neighborhood, eating the same food, at the same time, in the same room are a portrait in contrast. On one side of the room the KIPP students, all but two in attendance, are seated in order and eat while they talk in quiet, conversational tones. On the other side of the room, chaos is breaking out. Although a full third of the local school students are missing, lunch monitors scream at the children through bull horns, desperately trying to maintain control.

Because of its radically different setting, KIPP in New York has made significant departures in style from its sister school in Houston (see p. 93). The achievement of both schools, however, is clearly the result of dedicated teaching and instructional innovation. KIPP's phenomenal success in mathematics, for example, is the work of Frank Corcoran, who came with Levin from Houston to found the new academy. No textbook on the market today teaches math concepts in the sequence they are taught at KIPP.

And then there's the music.

Outside of academics, the string orchestra is the centerpiece of KIPP in New York. In the past few years the orchestra's reputation for excellence has helped the school raise over $70,000 to outfit its students with violas, violins, cellos, basses, and an array of percussion instruments. Everyone in the school studies music. Everyone plays in the orchestra. For Levin, the decision to stress music was simple. In music, concentration, dedication, and teamwork give rise to beauty and harmony. Music reveals the path to success.

KIPP demonstrates what is possible. But both Feinberg in Texas and Levin in New York believe that to replicate KIPP on a national scale, they would require a pool of educators that does not exist today. "In two communities that have nothing in common but a group of children abandoned by the establishment, we have opened schools that work," says Levin. "But what we do isn't easy. First, we need to find a way to make this level of commitment the standard. Then we need to make it attractive, livable, and affordable for teachers."

Notes:

75. California Achievement Test-5, Spring 1998. Provided by the New York City Board of Education Division of Assessment and Accountability.

Thomas E. Williams

Healthy Start Academy
515 Dowd Street
Durham, NC 27701
919.956.5599

A former assistant district superintendent in New York, Tom Williams opened his charter school in July 1997 with 135 students. The school was designed to serve needy minority children who qualify for many social services. The school has more than tripled in size in two years. Ninety-nine percent of Healthy Start students are black. Eighty percent qualify for the free or reduced-price lunch. Seventy-five percent come from single-parent homes. But academics remains the sole focus of its principal. "We're a school, not a welfare program," Williams says without apology. "We're not all things to all people. We're teachers for children who need us." At Healthy Start, Williams says achievement is the name of the game.

Last year, for example, the 1st grade scored in the 48th percentile. In response, the 1st grade teachers threw out their curriculum and focused exclusively on math and reading. This year's class, now in the 2nd grade, scored in the 99th percentile in all subjects. Last year's 2nd grade scored in the 71st percentile. Not happy with that result, the grade-level teachers also made some changes. This year's class, now 3rd graders, scored in the 81st percentile on the total battery.[77]

Grades: K-4
Students: 430
% Low-income: 80
Median Percentile in Reading: 88
Median Percentile in Math: 91[76]

Williams describes Healthy Start as a diagnostic prescriptive school. Testing is at the center of school life, because testing drives achievement. All children are first tracked according to their abilities based on the results of a threefold assessment: the Riverside 3Rs diagnostic test, the IBM/McGraw-Hill reading exam, and the Saxon math assessment. With those results in hand, educators at Healthy Start develop a Personalized Education Program for each student. Five parent conferences a year and five report cards track each child according to a portfolio of needs based on the results of the Iowa Test of Basic Skills.

Notes:

76. Iowa Test of Basic Skills, Spring 1999. Provided by Healthy Start Academy.
77. *Ibid.*

"It's one of our primary goals to prove that we can educate our children at a much higher level for less than what the state charges," Williams says. Healthy Start receives $3,400 per child from the state and $1,890 per child from the county. Despite its large population of low-income students, the school only receives $60,000 in Title I funds and purposely does not seek federal grant money. The school is housed in a 75-year-old building that was close to uninhabitable when classes opened. Through keen fiscal management, Williams has already plowed $100,000 into refurbishing his building.

Williams invests most of his time and money in his staff. He personally trains all 25 of his teachers and every morning at 7:30 he meets with a different grade-level teaching team for its weekly conference. The school is open for eleven months, July to June, with only a two-week break for Christmas.

"We can pay our teachers more because it's not getting siphoned off by a central office," Williams says. Teachers at Healthy Start receive $31,000 for starters and $35,000 if they have a master's degree. By contrast, public schools in the region pay $22,000 for first-year teachers. Healthy Start also contributes an additional 8 percent of a teacher's annual salary to individually managed retirement accounts. At the end of the year, merit-based bonuses range from $1,000 to $2,000 per teacher. "All of this compares to the public schools *taking* 6 percent from their teachers," Williams retorts.

In July 1999 Williams opened Research Triangle Academy, a K-4 school for 150 children, which has the capacity to grow to 800 students in three years. Williams also plans to open four or five more schools under his direction with individual principals to run them locally. "We'll give you the best service in the state for the lowest price in town. Boy, are we going to make some people angry," he chuckles.

Angelo F. Milicia

Stephen Girard/GAMP
18th Street and Snyder Ave.
Philadelphia, PA 19145
215.952.8554

Named after the nineteenth-century shipping magnate and philanthropist Stephen Girard, this local neighborhood elementary school (K-4) of almost 700 children is attached to a gifted music and humanities program for grades 5 through 12 that draws from all over the city. The Girard Academic Music Program, or GAMP as it is known, serves approximately 250 students in the middle school and another 250 at the high school 'evel. Although admission to GAMP is based on certain performance requirements and the number of openings available, more than 80 percent of all the children in the two schools come from low-income families.

Angelo Milicia, now in his fourth year as the principal of the combined school, says that the upper school's emphasis on the arts has an excellent effect on the whole school's academic achievement. "All of our programs are instructional in nature and support the academic goals of the school," Milicia explains. "Oftentimes students of low-income families lack a rich background of experiences. Here they get active teaching and learning environments that fill the void and are culturally rich." His scores prove it. This year the middle school brought in

Grades: K-12
Students: 1,186
% Low-income: 82
Median Percentile in Reading: 66
Median Percentile in Math: 63[78]

the best results. The 7th grade scored in the 78th percentile in reading and the 70th in math, while the 8th graders scored in the 81st and 77th percentiles, respectively.[79]

Although students can study music for up to eight years in the magnet program, GAMP is not a performing arts school. Four years of music theory is required of everyone, but proficiency on a musical instrument is not. However rich the musical offerings might be, the academic program at GAMP follows a college preparatory curriculum that encourages

Notes:

78. Stanford-9 Achievement Test, Spring 1999. Provided by the School District of Philadelphia Office of Assessment. These scores are only for grades 7, 8, 10, and 11: the grades tested for local accountability purposes.
79. *Ibid.*

a wide choice of study in the liberal arts. But the expectations are also very clearly spelled out. In the high school, four years of English, math, science, and social science and two years of either Spanish or Italian are compulsory for graduation. Most seniors take Advanced Placement courses in American history and music theory. Every senior takes either calculus or pre-calculus. All go to college.

"These kids need to have a desire to come here," says Milicia. "But they don't always come fully proficient. Desire and aptitude are more important." Because of the school's interest in performance, the students understand that they must be able to demonstrate what they have learned. In the classical liberal tradition, this leads to a "talkative" and intellectual environment that puts a premium on good conversation and higher-order thinking skills. "Unlike most schools, the longer they're here, the better off they do," Milicia notes. Last year, the 60 children in the graduating class received over $1.5 million in scholarships.

Girard/GAMP is small by Philadelphia standards, but Milicia believes that even smaller is better. In order to provide the most individual instruction possible, he organized the school vertically into multiple grade-level clusters (K-4, 5-8, 9-12), or "learning communities," of 120 to 130 children each. "Success across the board is a tall order, but small learning communities can make it a reality," says Milicia. Teachers in these clusters are also grouped together into instructional support teams that improve each other's teaching and accelerate the learning of students from year to year.

Like so many other high-performing principals, Milicia puts a premium on testing: "Assessment drives instruction. If the kids aren't tested regularly, how are we to know what they need? And standards drive assessment. If we don't know where they're going, how will we get them there?"

For the past 26 years, Milicia has worked as a teacher and principal in high-poverty schools. The failure of most low-income schools, he says, is a simple failure to encourage achievement. "I was originally a teacher of children in the projects," he recalls. "The experienced teachers thought the kids were animals. I was told they couldn't be taught. But through drill and practice, they learned, and they learned to be successful." Before coming to Girard/GAMP, Milicia was the principal of Andrew Jackson, another low-income school in Philadelphia, which was ranked second out of 44 in the district when he left.

Milicia maintains that in many schools children fall through the cracks because no one is held personally responsible for their success. He says, "Here, I'm responsible."

Vivian C. Dillihunt

Rozelle Elementary
993 Roland Street
Memphis, TN 38114
901.722.4612

Memphis City Schools is the largest school system in the state of Tennessee and the 20th largest metropolitan school system in the United States. Eighty-two percent of all the public school children in the city come from low-income families. The median percentile ranking of its 166 schools combined is below the 35th percentile in reading.[80] Yet, amid these dire numbers, in a part of south Memphis called Annesdale, an elementary school for the creative and performing arts is turning hard work and innovation into real opportunity for hundreds of children.

In 1994 Memphis School Superintendent Gerry House decided that every school in the system would adopt one of eighteen whole-school reform models that met the specific needs of its local community. Rozelle Elementary, a neighborhood school that is 99 percent black and 88 percent low-income, was one of the first 35 schools to enter the program. After merging the school's creative and performing arts curriculum with the Modern Red Schoolhouse reform model (see Appendix A), principal Vivian Dillihunt quickly established Rozelle's reputation for excellence. In 1998, the 3rd and 4th grades, for example, scored at or above the 80th percentile on the language portion of the Terra Nova achievement test.[82]

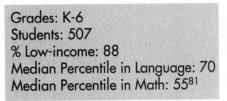

Grades: K-6
Students: 507
% Low-income: 88
Median Percentile in Language: 70
Median Percentile in Math: 55[81]

Dillihunt says that Rozelle's success stems from two things: its teachers and their teaching.

When she arrived in 1994, Dillihunt instituted a comprehensive professional development program centered on instructional strategies, curriculum preparation, and teaching to standards. "We don't always get the best teachers," says Dillihunt, a former instructional supervisor. "We

Notes:

80. *21st Century Schools Report Card*, Memphis City 1997. Provided by the Tennessee Department of Education, Research and Evaluation Office.
81. TCAP Achievement Test (Terra Nova), Spring 1998. Provided by Memphis City Schools, Office of Research and Evaluation.
82. *Ibid.*

take what we get and turn them into the best teachers through training, teamwork, and mentoring."

At Rozelle, all teachers work in teams to meet the goals of the school. Not only does this teamwork help maintain consistency across the school's Core Knowledge curriculum, but it also keeps the school focused on achievement. "No one is allowed to fail unless they want to fail," says Dillihunt. Teamwork, in fact, extends to all aspects of the program. Because the teachers at Rozelle are responsible for the design and implementation of the school's curriculum, they are also directly involved in determining how the school's funds are spent. According to Dillihunt, this is one of the most important freedoms of site-based management models, because it invites a new degree of care and concern that comes primarily with ownership. And in order to *maintain* this cooperative environment among the faculty, teachers at Rozelle participate in the interview process and "buy into the new teachers," as Dillihunt says.

"What we teach can be taught to any children anywhere," says Dillihunt. In addition to the basic skills emphasized in the Core Knowledge curriculum, children at Rozelle can study dance, art, creative writing, and music at the primary and intermediate levels. While this emphasis on the arts helps to create both an intellectually charged and nurturing environment, which Dillihunt says is beneficial to the education of all children, again, she attributes the quality of the environment to her teachers. "All of my teachers have a love for children and a desire to teach," she says. While this may not be true of some schools, it is a prerequisite at Rozelle. "Bad teachers do not stay at Rozelle," Dillihunt says. "Teachers work together in every phase of our program. Peer pressure causes those who do not want to succeed to leave."

Michael Feinberg

KIPP Academy
7120 Beechnut
Houston, TX 77074
713.541.2561

"There are no shortcuts." This simple motto is the heart of the KIPP Academy in Houston. Nine-and-a-half hour days, class on Saturday, school during the summer, and more than two hours of homework each night are all non-negotiable. KIPP teaches that if you want to succeed in life, then you have to work hard in school. And KIPP delivers on its promise.

For the past four years, 5th graders—who typically come to KIPP with 50-percent passing rates on the Texas Assessment of Academic Skills—have jumped to over 90 percent passing in both math and reading in their first year at the school.[84] After a student's first year, KIPP has virtually a 100 percent passing rate in all grades and all disciplines, making it the highest performing of the 38 middle schools in the Houston Independent School District. Many of its students are the children of immigrant workers who come from the Gulfton area of southwest Houston. Almost the entire school qualifies for the free or reduced-price lunch; 90 percent are Hispanic.

Grades: 5-9
Students: 270
% Low-income: 95
Median Percentile in Reading: 61
Median Percentile in Math: 81[83]

Michael Feinberg and David Levin (now principal of KIPP Academy in the Bronx) were two Teach for America teachers whose success with their middle school students in Houston was compromised after the children left their classrooms. Like so many poor urban children, their students were prey to drugs, gangs, and a cycle of despair. In order to break that cycle, Feinberg and Levin made college the goal. In 1994 they started the

Notes:

83. Stanford-9 Achievement Test, December 1998. Provided by KIPP Academy.
84. Provided by KIPP Academy based on the Texas Education Agency Academic Excellence Indicator System. These gains vary from year to year depending on the incoming students' prior rates of progress. The 1998 6th grade class, for example, had a passing rate of 35 and 33 percent on math and reading as incoming 5th graders. The next year, that same class had 93 and 92 percent passing rates. In 1998, 100 percent of the class passed in math and 97 percent in reading.

Knowledge Is Power Program (KIPP) out of a single classroom in Garcia Elementary as an academically rigorous college preparatory program for 5th graders. Now a charter school that has plans to establish other schools under its direction, KIPP is located on a campus of twelve trailers parked just beyond the baseball fields of Houston Baptist University.

Time on task is sacred at KIPP. "If you're off the bus, you're working," says Feinberg, the no-nonsense director of the school whose boyish grin clashes oddly with his shaven head and six-foot-four frame. His charm is equally disarming; he is clearly liked by his students. Casually uniformed children wearing tee-shirts indicating their class year wave to him as they hustle from trailer to trailer cycling through the various disciplines of the school's liberal arts curriculum. "What year are you going to college?" Feinberg calls out to the 5th graders around him. In unison they cry at the top of their lungs, "2006!"

All told, KIPPsters spend 67 percent more time in the classroom than the average public school student.[85] Each morning students receive a worksheet of math, logic, and word problems for them to solve in the free minutes that appear throughout the day. "We wanted the kids to do something while we checked their work, so we came up with the worksheets," Feinberg explains. "It's all a work in progress. You have to come up with ways to meet your needs and constantly improve your teaching. We're every bit a school for teachers as we are a school for students."

Before founding KIPP, Feinberg and Levin scoured the country for the best teaching practices available, hoping that by studying success they could best replicate it. The work of Rafe Esquith, the 1992 Disney Teacher of the Year, has been so inspirational to Feinberg and Levin that KIPP still underwrites the travel costs of any teacher who wishes to visit him at Hobart Elementary in Los Angeles. As another example, the spectacular gains that KIPP students make in their first year is in part the result of a dynamic teaching method that Feinberg and Levin learned from Harriet Ball, a teacher from Houston. Singing songs choreographed with movements to aid their memorization, the children quickly learn the math and language concepts they need to catch up with their peers. "We then take that success and make it a way of life," Feinberg remarks.

Feinberg maintains, however, that no one teaching method is responsible for the school's achievement. Rather, the whole KIPP framework is built around maximizing teaching time and teacher accountability.

Notes:

85. This figure assumes the average public middle school student is in class 180 days a year from 8 A.M. to 3 P.M. with a half-hour break for lunch and another for recess.

Teachers are free to teach as they see fit, but they are personally accountable to the director of the school for the individual progress of their students. "We put no limits on what teachers can do here," Feinberg says. "But their signed commitment to excellence makes them morally and contractually obligated to see that their students succeed. They know they *have* to teach until the kids get it."

KIPP students, parents, and teachers all sign a commitment "to do whatever it takes to learn." Teachers carry cellphones with toll-free numbers and are on call 24 hours a day to answer any concerns their students might have. "Ten calls a night might sound like a drag," says Feinberg, "but everyone goes to bed ready for school the next day."

Between the signed contract and the rigorous expectations of the program, Feinberg believes that his parents have made a deal with him. "I can go to them if I need help with their children. In exchange, they can come to me if they need help keeping the roof over their heads." KIPP faculty regularly visit students in their homes and—when necessary—teach parents the importance of checking their children's homework, reading with them, and supporting their college aspirations. And yes, the school also holds workshops on home ownership.

Success in the classroom at KIPP is now coming home to benefit its families in very tangible ways. Last year's 8th grade class—the first class of youngsters to go through the school from start to finish—received over $1 million in scholarships to attend the schools of their choice.

Wilma B. Rimes

Mabel B. Wesley Elementary
800 Dillard Street
Houston, TX 77091
713.696.2860

Mabel B. Wesley Elementary, named after a former slave girl turned school principal and educational advocate, is one of the longest running success stories documented in these pages. Despite fierce political opposition, accusations of cheating, and blatant attempts to compromise the school, for more than 20 years this charter elementary has been among the best in Houston. Located in a very poor part of the city called Acres Homes, Wesley is approximately 92 percent black, 7 percent Hispanic, and 1 percent white. The school's record of achievement has gained a national reputation including, most recently, the attention of the Oprah Winfrey Show.

In 1998, 100 percent of the 3rd graders passed the reading portion of the Texas state assessment test. In the 5th grade, 97 percent passed in reading and 94 percent passed in math.[87] On the national exams the results are also impressive. Last year the kindergarten and the 1st grade scored in the 80th percentile in reading. Almost half of the 5th grade scored in the top quartile in the nation in math.[88] This level of excellence was not always so.

When Thaddeus S. Lott became principal at Wesley in 1975, most of the students read several years below grade level, many were non-readers, even many 6th graders were completely illiterate. In response, Lott installed a school-wide Direct Instruction (DI) language arts curriculum and soon after implemented direct instruction programs for all subject areas. By 1979, students in the 3rd, 4th, and 5th grades were performing almost two years ahead of the pre-DI students. By

Grades: PK-5
Students: 1,066
% Low-income: 87
Median Percentile in Reading: 61
Median Percentile in Math: 66[86]

Notes:

86. Stanford-9 Achievement Test, Spring 1999. Provided by Wesley Elementary.
87. Texas Assessment of Academic Skills, 1998. Provided by the Texas Education Agency Academic Excellence Indicator System. See *http://www.tea.state.tx.us.*
88. Stanford-9 Achievement Test, Spring 1999. Provided by Wesley Elementary.

1986, almost the entire school was scoring two years *above* grade level.[89] "It's a myth that if you're born in a poor community and your skin is a certain color that you can't achieve on a higher level," says Lott.

"There are several keys to our success," says Wilma Rimes, who became the principal of Wesley five years ago. "A research-based curriculum, ongoing teacher training, and an administration that accepts no excuses for student failure are all a part of it. Although our academic standards reflect the state's desired outcomes, merely passing is not acceptable to us. Our standard is based on the highest expectations for everyone, no matter what their socio-economic circumstances."

All instruction at Wesley is clearly and explicitly taught. Rimes says this simple fact, and the school's emphasis on reading, accounts for most of its success. "While many other schools changed programs as educational fads shifted, we stayed with and perfected our program. We're down to the fine tuning while a nation of teachers can't teach reading." Rimes stresses the importance of language acquisition and development, in particular: phonics in pre-kindergarten and kindergarten, explicit instruction in sound/spelling correspondence, systematic teaching of regular sound/spelling relationships, and a strong literature component to teach comprehension.

For many years, Wesley did not receive the support of the central district administration. Rimes explains, "Various efforts were made to stop the success of the school's teaching methods, which were neither 'whole language' nor 'developmentally appropriate.' But 'developmentally appropriate' [to central administration] only means a black child has no business learning how to read." In more recent years Wesley has received significant support from Rod Paige, the first black superintendent of the Houston Independent School District.

The irony, says Rimes, is that today a school can become a center of learning simply by demanding basic skills. Through incentive programs encouraging all kinds of outside reading, most Wesley students have mastered the basic skills in reading by the end of kindergarten. Almost half of the 2nd graders read at a 4th-grade level, can subtract seven-digit numbers, and proofread a paragraph for grammar, spelling, and capitalization. "The teachers' colleges are to blame for so much school failure," Rimes says. "If they would just teach teaching methods, more schools could get these results."

Notes:

89. Gary L. Adams and Siegfried Engelmann, *Research on Direct Instruction: 25 Years Beyond DISTAR*. (Seattle: Educational Achievement Systems, 1996), p. 100.

Approximately 65 percent of Wesley's teachers have fewer than five years of experience. On-site coaching and continuous teacher training makes it possible for even the newest teachers to be highly effective. Rimes and her assistant principal observe classes daily, looking for the specific skills their teachers need to develop. Throughout the year individualized training is provided, based on the needs of each teacher, and the test results of her students. "Everything here is data driven," says Rimes. "Teacher performance will remain the same year after year if you do not customize a teacher's training to meet her specific weaknesses or needs."

Most alumni from Wesley go on to the magnet schools in Houston or to the city's most prestigious private academies such as Kinkaid and the John Cooper School. As for the teachers, the success of the school is its own reward and makes for a loyal, passionate, and dedicated staff. Because Wesley teachers are actively recruited by other schools and districts, some teachers choose to take their talents elsewhere. But as Rimes says proudly, "If you teach at Wesley a few years, you can write your ticket anywhere."

Appendix A
Educational Reform Models

Core Knowledge: is an elementary and middle school program that insists upon a solid, specific, shared core curriculum in order to help children establish strong foundations in all the basic skills across all subject areas. Starting in kindergarten, students learn basic facts in various subjects including: language arts, history, geography, math, science, and the fine arts. Teachers at each grade level are expected to follow the same curriculum in order to establish a core understanding of each subject and to guarantee a mastery of the principal facts and skills required to participate in each successive grade. The sequence that Core Knowledge specifies was chosen from extensive research into the content and structure of the highest-performing elementary school systems around the world.

Developed by E.D. Hirsch, Jr., a professor of English literature at the University of Virginia, the program was first commercially available in 1990. Ten years later, the program is now offered in 950 school systems in 46 states. Hirsch subsequently founded the Core Knowledge Foundation, a non-profit organization that researches curricula and develops learning materials that aid and extend the offerings of the program.

Many disadvantaged children have exceptional difficulty learning to read and write. Extensive research has found that many of these children lack a basic core of knowledge that enables them to attach new information to what they already know. Core Knowledge is particularly appealing to low-income schools for two primary reasons: 1) Most low-income children are not exposed to many learning opportunities outside of the classroom. Because of the depth and range of its academic offerings, Core Knowledge supplements this need and helps all children gain a better understanding of the world around them. 2) Low-income schools often have a high mobility rate, that is, a large percentage of the children enter or leave the school in a single year. With different schools teaching different material in an arbitrary context and sequence, high mobility rates quickly lead to large learning gaps. Like any other common curriculum, Core Knowledge is designed to insure that each grade in every school is taught the same material in the same sequence. When children transfer, their education remains uninterrupted.

The first three years of Core Knowledge include a minimum of five days of training and three site visits for $15,000 per year for a school with up to 25 staff members. Schools are charged a one-time materials fee of $50 per student. The Core Knowledge Foundation encourages schools to budget between $200 and $500 per teacher to purchase additional resources for the classroom.

Direct Instruction: is a highly structured, highly interactive instructional approach designed to accelerate the learning of all students. Through scripted lesson plans that are delivered in rapid sequence to small groups of children grouped by performance level, Direct Instruction (DI) aims to move all students through the curriculum at the fastest possible pace while guaranteeing mastery at every level.

Formerly called Direct Instruction System for Teaching and Remediation (DISTAR), DI was first developed by Siegfried Engelmann thirty years ago. In the late '60s, Project Follow Through—one of the nation's largest educational experiments that tested nine different school models over the course of eight years as a part of President Johnson's War on Poverty—found Direct Instruction the most successful in driving student achievement.

Instead of creating their own lesson plans, DI teachers follow exact scripts when teaching. According to the Association for Direct Instruction, scripted lessons increase the learning efficiency of a class. The scripted lessons are a result of extensive empirical investigation into the design and delivery of instruction and are revised based on specific student errors taken from field tests. Students who progress faster than the rest of the group are identified and further accelerated based on their rates of progress. Students who progress more slowly are also identified, grouped together, and instructed in a way that provides opportunity for faster learning at their skill level.

Schools can implement Direct Instruction for one or all subjects. Several commercial providers are available. These providers also offer on-site teacher training. First year reading, for example, for a school with 400 students and eighteen teachers can cost $78,000 or $195 per student. This total includes an estimated $38,000 for materials and $40,000 for training. Schools can also install the program with no outside support. Schools have to purchase required curriculum materials as well as presentation books that provide instructions for monitoring student progress. Materials are published by SRA/McGraw Hill and can be used however the school chooses. High-performing schools recommend using outside help in the start-up phase.

Modern Red Schoolhouse: is a whole school reform model that aids higher achievement among students by streamlining instruction and by deploying school resources specifically to meet the academic needs of students. In this model, site-based management promotes school autonomy and puts the school's management in the service of improved instruction. Like the schoolhouse of old, the model shares across all schools a common set of academic standards. It is modern in its use of time, diversity of teaching techniques, and deployment of technology.

Developed by the Hudson Institute and sponsored by New American Schools, Modern Red Schoolhouse began entering schools in 1993. Six tenets form the basis of the design. 1) Standards and Assessment. Schools need to set standards in core academic subjects with an emphasis on high levels of academic achievement for all students. 2) Culture. Students should also have the discipline of mind and character to be contributing members of a democratic society. 3) Organization. Schools are free to organize instruction and deploy resources as they see fit, so long as they are held accountable through regular testing of student progress. 4) Accountability. Decentralized decision making requires clear expectations and accountability for meeting those expectations. 5) Technology. All students must be familiar with today's computer and telecommunications technology. 6) Choice. Schools should be places where students and staff members choose to belong.

Modern Red Schoolhouse requires students to master their subjects before they progress to the next level. Instead of 12 grades, this model separates children into three divisions: primary, intermediate, and upper. The developers recommend using the Core Knowledge curriculum, but under this reform model teachers have the freedom to use other curricula or their own innovative teaching methods whenever they wish.

The first-year cost of implementing Modern Red Schoolhouse is $215,000. This cost includes training, technical assistance, and the cost of technology. After that, an average school of 500 students can expect to pay $60,000 to $80,000 per year for three years of implementation. For this fee, each year schools receive 30 days of training and consulting.

Success for All: is a program that is designed to ensure that every child learns how to read. Developed by Robert Slavin and Nancy Madden at

Johns Hopkins University, the program is geared for students of urban areas who are "at-risk" for school failure. First piloted in 1987, the program is now installed in over 1,100 schools nationwide. Although Success for All is designed just for reading, its sister program, Roots and Wings, expands to other subject areas.

Success for All begins by teaching pre-kindergarten and kindergarten students oral language skills. To become more familiar with stories and words, students listen, retell, and act out stories. According to the developers, this allows the young students to recognize common words and to become aware of the different sounds that make a given word. Reading groups are a key feature that require all students, usually up to the 4th grade, to read for 90 minutes each day. Students are grouped by their reading performance level. Curriculum-based assessments are administered every eight weeks. Students who fall behind receive specialized tutoring for 20 minutes each day from a certified tutor. High-performing students are regrouped with other students who have demonstrated a similar level of mastery.

A program facilitator at each school is needed to oversee the details of implementation. In addition, the facilitator is a liaison between the staff and the family. Help from the family is essential to students developing reading skills. As part of the Success for All program, a family support team is set up that consists of the facilitator, parents, counselors, principal, and other school staff.

According to the Success for All Foundation, implementing this program for the first year costs on average $75,000. The second year costs $26,000 and $20,000 for the third. These costs include training, materials, follow-up visits, and other services. Cost can vary depending on the size of the school and the resources available.

Roots and Wings: Developed by Robert Slavin and Nancy Madden of Johns Hopkins University, Roots and Wings was created to be used in conjunction with Success for All. Roots and Wings first seeks to ensure that every child will successfully complete elementary school. Secondly it endeavors to "engage students in activities so that they can learn the usefulness and interconnectedness of all knowledge." Two major parts of its curriculum are "MathWings" and "WorldLab," which emphasize student-led, collective learning exercises. Roots and Wings uses the Success for All reading curriculum, which provides extensive instruction, continual assessment, and special tutoring in reading.

Appendix B
Research Summaries

Portraits of Six Benchmark Schools: Diverse Approaches
to Improving Student Performance
Gordon Cawelti
Educational Research Service (1999)
69 pages

These case studies, prepared by one of the most respected names in the business, are exceedingly well done and a welcome addition to the study of schools that serve low-income children.

Cawelti's research begins with a simple question: "Are there schools that are getting good results even though they serve kids who are tough to teach"? Like *No Excuses*, Cawelti concludes: "All students can learn, provided that we give them the right educational environment."

The six schools profiled in this study are: Frederick Douglass Academy (New York, NY), Carl C. Waitz Elementary (Mission, TX), Exeter High School (Ajax, Ontario), James Madison Elementary (Pittsburgh, PA), Clay Elementary (Clay, WV), and Dodge-Edison Elementary (Wichita, KS).

Relying upon classroom observations and interviews with administrators, teachers, students, and parents, Cawelti identifies five characteristics—common to all six of the schools—that contribute to their academic growth and success:
- A focus on clear standards and improving results
- Teamwork helps ensure accountability
- The principal is a strong educational leader
- Teachers are deeply committed to helping all students achieve
- Multiple changes are made to improve the instructional life of students

Dispelling the Myth: High-Poverty Schools Exceeding Expectations
The Education Trust (1999)
102 pages

"Somewhere along the line," writes Kati Haycock, president of the Education Trust, "someone decided that poor children couldn't learn, or, at least, not at a very high level. And everyone fell in line." *Dispelling the Myth* presents survey data on 366 schools from 21 states that challenge this widespread prejudice.

With cooperation from the Council of Chief State School Officers and funding from the U.S. Department of Education, the Education Trust "constructed and administered a survey of 1,200 schools that had been identified by the states as their top scoring and/or most improving schools with poverty levels over 50 percent." Researchers then probed for common lessons that might benefit low-performing schools serving large populations of low-income children.

In summary, this report makes the following suggestions:
- Use state standards extensively to design curriculum and instruction, assess student work, and evaluate teachers.
- Increase instructional time in reading and math in order to help students meet standards.
- Devote a larger proportion of funds to support professional development focused on changing instructional practice.
- Implement comprehensive systems to monitor individual student progress and provide extra support to students as soon as it is needed.
- Focus efforts to involve parents on helping students meet standards.
- Have state or district accountability systems in place that have real consequences for adults in the schools.

Beating the Odds: High-Achieving Elementary Schools in High-Poverty Neighborhoods
Noreen Connell, Nancy Mendelow, Deborah Tyson
Educational Priorities Panel (1999)
94 pages

Of 669 New York City public elementary schools ranked in 1997 according to standardized test results, 261 served high-poverty communities, and 53 of these high-poverty schools performed "far above average" academically. *Beating the Odds* is a comprehensive discussion of local and system-wide reform recommendations based on practices culled from 14 of these 53 schools.

The research objective of *Beating the Odds*, commissioned by a coalition of local community and church organizations, was to "document practices that resulted in sustained high performance in neighborhoods where poorly functioning or mediocre schools are the norm."

Most of the policy recommendations made in this report concern funding disparities or are otherwise financial in nature. At the end, the report calls for an evaluation of current hiring procedures and practices to see whether they support a merit promotion system.

Hope for Urban Education
Joe Johnson
The Charles A. Dana Center, University of Texas at Austin (1999)
155 pages

In this series of case studies, Joe Johnson profiles nine high-performing, low-income schools in order to identify their effective practices. The nine schools are: Baskin Elementary (San Antonio, TX); Goodale Elementary (Detroit, MI); Lora B. Peck Elementary (Houston, TX); Centerville Elementary (East St. Louis, IL); Burgess Elementary (Atlanta, GA); James Ward Elementary (Chicago, IL); Baldwin Elementary (Boston, MA); Hawley Environmental (Milwaukee, WI); and Gladys Noon Spellman Elementary (Cheverly, MD).[90]

For each, Johnson provides the enrollment, attendance rate, grade span, ethnic breakdown, percentage of students with limited English proficiency, and percentage of students qualifying for free and reduced price lunches. Johnson also lists "key programs" said to be responsible, at least in part, for the schools' success. Canady Scheduling, Links to Literacy, Move-It Math, and Success for All are representative examples.

Each case study begins with a description of the school's atmosphere and physical plant. After that, the actual findings are largely reported in the form of teacher and administrator quotations. Although these case studies provide a wealth of interesting and useful data, Johnson offers little analysis beyond his concluding paragraphs entitled "Reflections of the Researchers." As a result, the reader is left to determine for himself the best practices common among these exemplary schools. What is more, the thematic subheadings differ from study to study making it hard to compare the schools and even harder to conclude what practices can be successfully interchanged.

These analytical shortcomings notwithstanding, Johnson's research provides powerful evidence that there is no excuse for the failure of

Notes:

90. See *http://starcenter.org/pdf/urbaned.pdf*.

most public schools to teach poor children. By implementing proven and effective practices, Johnson argues, schools can successfully educate all children.

Turning Around Low-Performing Schools:
A Guide for State and Local Leaders
U.S. Department of Education (1998)
68 pages

Produced by presidential directive, this guide recommends the following strategies for turning around low-performing schools:
- Raise academic standards.
- Promote accountability.
- Keep schools safe and free of drugs.
- Provide students with extra help when needed.
- Increase parental and community involvement.
- Recruit, prepare, and provide continuing training to teachers.
- Reward excellence in teaching.

The first section, aptly titled "Raising the Stakes," advocates setting high standards and holding schools and students accountable to them. The second and third sections, "Focus on Learning" and "Building School Capacity," further discuss strategies for improving student performance. Such strategies include improving curriculum and classroom instruction; building leadership, trust and ownership; and using performance data to drive continuous improvement. The final section explores intervention strategies, and school reconstitution in particular.

Although this report is supposedly based on the experience of several high-performing schools cited as case studies, its practical recommendations remain vague throughout. As a result, its suggestions are never formed into plans for action. The section devoted to reconstitution is particularly irresolute.

The bibliography represents a very good sampling of relevant research from 1991 to the present.

Raising Student Achievement: A Resource Guide
for Redesigning Low-Performing Schools
American Federation of Teachers (1997)
174 pages

To improve low-performing schools, this guide advocates policies which:
- Are grounded in high academic standards.
- Enforce high standards of behavior.

- Use criteria for the identification of low-performing schools that are clear and understood by all stakeholders.
- Address the particular needs of the individual school.
- Are backed by solid research.
- Involve staff and provide them with the professional development, time, and resources they will need to be effective.

Raising Student Achievement is divided into four sections. The first describes the reform efforts of three AFT affiliates in Dade County, New York City, and San Francisco. The second and third offer guidelines for implementing change and profile research-based programs proven to raise student achievement. The fourth reproduces contract language from agreements negotiated by AFT affiliates that maintain "the delicate balance between the need for dramatic improvement and the rights of school staff affected by change."

Successful Texas Schoolwide Programs
Laura Klein, Joseph Johnson, and Mary Ragland
The Charles A. Dana Center, University of Texas at Austin (1997)
18 pages

Klein, Johnson, and Ragland, with financial backing from the U.S. Department of Education, suggest that "there is good reason to be hopeful about the education of students who attend public schools in poor communities." Indeed, "schools where almost all students live in low-income situations can be schools in which almost all students achieve high levels of academic success."

These researchers identified over 50 high-performing, high-poverty schools in Texas that met the following criteria: 1) over 60 percent of students received free or reduced-price lunches, 2) the school received Title I funds and implemented schoolwide Title I programs, and 3) at least 70 percent of students passed the reading and mathematics sections of the Texas Assessment of Academic Skills (TAAS).

This is a valuable study that might have been significantly improved by a tighter focus on the specific practices of the schools profiled. Although its general findings are well presented, the reader longs for more detail. Because of resource limitations, only 26 schools were included in the final survey. Those schools are: Adams Elementary (Cleburne), Apple Springs Elementary (Apple Springs), Boys Ranch High (Boys Ranch), T.A. Brown Elementary (Austin), Kate Burgess Elementary (Wichita Falls), C.F. Carr Elementary (Dallas), Cisco Elementary (Cisco), East Side Elementary (San Felipe-Del Rio), El Magnet at Zavala Elementary (Ector County), A.G. Hilliard Elementary (North

Forest), Hueco Elementary (Socorro), R.L. Isaacs Elementary (Houston), Lamar Elementary (Corpus Christi), Los Fresnos Intermediate (Los Fresnos), Leo Marcell Elementary (Mission), Nixon-Smiley Middle (Nixon-Smiley), Lucille Pearson Elementary (Mission), L.R. Pietzsch Elementary (Beaumont), Sagamore Hill Elementary (Fort Worth), E.J. Scott Elementary (Houston), Annie Sims Elementary (Mount Pleasant), Springlake Junior High (Springlake-Earth), Sunrise Elementary (Amarillo), Three Way School (Three Way), West Avenue Elementary (North East), and George C. Wolffarth Elementary (Lubbock).

Schools That Work: Educating Disadvantaged Children
William J. Bennett
U.S. Department of Education (1987)
90 pages

Schools That Work is the best report of its kind. Packed with helpful examples and practical insights, this no-nonsense guide to real education reform unequivocally proclaims, "the notion that poverty and bad schools are inevitably linked is a prescription for inaction. It is a self-fulfilling prophecy of despair and it is flat out-wrong." Although much of its data is outdated today, *Schools That Work* offers the best bibliography of research available through 1986.

Appropriately, Bennett champions education reform within the larger context of social reform. Better educated youth, he argues, are better citizens and far less likely later to find themselves on welfare or in jail.

Citing positive reform efforts in 23 schools, *Schools That Work* departs slightly from the typical case-study methodology. Instead of profiling the schools themselves, this report makes 16 recommendations for improving the educational outcomes of low-income children while citing a representative policy or program from one of the 23 outstanding schools.

The 16 recommendations are:
- Mobilize students, staff, and parents around a vision of a school in which all students can achieve.
- Create an orderly and safe school environment by setting high standards for discipline and attendance.
- Help students acquire the habits and attitudes necessary for progress in school and in later life.
- Provide a challenging academic curriculum.
- Tailor instructional strategies to the needs of disadvantaged children.

- Help students with limited English proficiency become proficient and comfortable in the English language—speaking, reading, and writing—as soon as possible.
- Focus early childhood programs on disadvantaged children to increase their chances for success.
- Reach out to help parents take part in educating their children.
- Instill in children the values they need to progress in school and throughout life.
- Demand the best from children and show this concern by supervising children's progress.
- Get involved with the schools and with children's education outside school
- Invest in the education and future success of disadvantaged children.
- Ensure that education reforms make a difference for disadvantaged students.
- Give local school officials sufficient authority to act quickly, decisively, and creatively to improve schools, and hold them accountable for results.
- Assess the results of school practices, paying special attention to the impact of reform on disadvantaged students.
- Support improved education for disadvantaged students through supplementary and compensatory programs, leadership, and research.

Appendix C
Suggested Titles for Further Reading

Adler, Mortimer J. *The Paideia Proposal.* New York: Macmillan Publishing Co., 1982.

This short little manifesto is perhaps the most succinct statement to date outlining why we have public schools, what they are to teach, and how we can properly reform them. If we are to improve the opportunities of our youth, the prospects of our economy, and the viability of our democratic institutions, then we must believe that all children are truly educable and deserving of the very best schooling available.

American Institutes for Research. *An Educators' Guide to Schoolwide Reform.* Virginia:Educational Research Service, 1999.

This guide, assembled by the American Institutes for Research in association with the American Federation of Teachers, National Educators Association, National Association of Elementary School Principals, and the National Association of Secondary School Principals, provides some much-needed hard data on various school reform strategies. Designed to help educators decide which methods best meet the needs of their local schools, this is an admirable effort that should gain wide circulation for its clear presentation and ease of use. Among the 24 schoolwide reform approaches that it presents, only eight have demonstrated 'strong' or 'promising' evidence of positive effects on student achievement.

Burtless, Gary, ed. *Does Money Matter?* Washington, DC: The Brookings Institution, 1996.

This compilation of essays examines whether spending disparities between schools affect student performance or a student's future earning potential. The various studies report conflicting findings on the effects of school spending on student outcomes: Although school spending is found to have no significant impact on student achievement while a student is in school, higher levels of spending are said to have a beneficial effect on future earnings.

Mathews, Jay. *Escalante*. New York: Henry Holt and Company, 1988.
    Jaime Escalante's extraordinary teaching career illustrates that low-income, inner-city, minority students can succeed at the highest levels in school when an outstanding teacher drives their achievement. Through his brilliant teaching techniques and single-minded commitment to academic excellence, Escalante made a national powerhouse out of a defunct mathematics program at Garfield High in East Los Angeles. In 1987, Garfield's Advanced Placement Calculus Program was ranked among the top ten in the United States.

Mayer, Susan E. *What Money Can't Buy*. Cambridge: Harvard University Press, 1997.
    Contradicting both her personal politics and earlier social research, Mayer's book represents a revolutionary assessment of the relationship between parental income and the life chances of children. Although additional parental income does improve a child's chances for success, Mayer demonstrates that parental income is not as important to children's outcomes as many social scientists have previously thought. Parental characteristics that employers value such as honesty, diligence, and reliability also improve children's life chances, independent of their effect on parents' income. In particular, her work speaks volumes to policies and procedures that would try to improve educational outcomes simply through reallocating financial resources.

Monroe, Lorraine. *Nothing's Impossible*. New York: Public Affairs, 1997.
    Lorraine Monroe, founder of the Frederick Douglass Academy in Harlem, recounts the tremendous dedication and innovative teaching that made her school one of the most dramatic turn-around stories in the history of urban education. Recalling examples from her own educational formation, Monroe outlines the essential elements of a successful school in what she calls her "Monroe Doctrine." These observations, coupled with her more specific advice for administrators, provide an excellent introduction to that same no-nonsense approach to basic schooling that made Frederick Douglass a success story.

Ravitch, Diane and Joseph P. Viteritti, eds. *New Schools for a New Century*. New Haven: Yale University Press, 1997.

This compilation of essays on school reform examines a number of institutional problems facing American, inner-city schools today. Two essays in particular are deserving of special attention:

- "Successful School-Based Management," by Priscilla Wohlstetter, Susan Albers Mohrman, and Peter J. Robertson, discusses whole-school reform methods as a remedy for ineffective, bureaucratic school systems. School-Based Management promotes change in the governance of school districts by decentralizing the nuclear administration. When teachers, parents, and school administrators have more control over the allocation of school resources, the authors argue, they are more likely to meet the immediate needs of their schoolchildren.

- "Somebody's Children," by Diane Ravitch, maintains that law makers and school officials must uphold genuine ideals of pluralism, equality, and excellence in education if successful schools are going to be available to all Americans. Ravitch argues for a means-tested choice program that would allow low-income students to attend better, smaller, and more autonomous schools.

Schlechty, Phillip C. *Inventing Better Schools*. San Francisco: Jossey-Bass Publishers, 1997.

Schlechty's study is a thoughtful handbook to school reform that focuses on the practical problems of implementing large-scale reforms into the everyday workings of a school. It is one thing to want high standards and rigorous assessments, it is another thing to bring them about. This book can help educators through that transition. Schlechty's focus on the student as a "customer of knowledge work" might not appeal to all, but it effectively communicates his vision of schooling as a service industry that stands much to gain from an increased attention to customer satisfaction. Ironically, he is not an advocate of privatizing schools. Through strategic planning—establishing a mission that provides an explicit course of action for the future—Schlechty maintains that our existing systems can bring about their own local reforms.

Stringfield, Sam, Steven Ross, and Lana Smith, eds. *Bold Plans for School Restructuring*. New Jersey: Lawrence Erlbaum Associates, 1996.

This book documents the first three years of the New American Schools Development Corporation, a consortium of national development teams that created nine of the most popular whole school reform models. Two of the programs highlighted in the book are Modern Red Schoolhouse and Roots and Wings.

Suskind, Ron. *A Hope in the Unseen: An American Odyssey from the Inner City to the Ivy League*. New York: Broadway Books, 1998.

This is the story of Cedric Jennings, a black youth from a single-parent, low-income home in Washington, D.C., who overcomes the anti-intellectual, gang-driven culture of his high school and enters Brown University on an academic scholarship. Suskind's reporting provides a rich, if at times disturbing, account of the many social, cultural, and academic hurdles that Jennings has to face even after he gains admission to Brown. In order for higher education to offer real opportunity and improved future prospects, so this story seems to argue, even our best efforts at the secondary level have to be much improved.

Appendix D
Definitions, Methods, and Procedure

The findings reported here are not the product of formal scientific research. Neither were the schools selected for this study chosen from a comprehensive survey of high-performing schools. At first, prospective schools were drawn from recommendations made by the Department of Education Blue Ribbon Schools Program. From this it was quickly determined that the schools recognized by that program rarely achieve the level of academic accomplishment required by this study. And because there is no single source that reports on the poverty and performance of all schools nationwide, a new approach was required.

After consulting with state education chiefs, their offices of assessment, state and local think tanks, teachers' unions, not-for-profit organizations supporting research in elementary and secondary education, family foundations providing financial support to outstanding high-poverty schools, educational consultants, and research organizations developing intervention programs for "at-risk" students, a list of just over 400 prospective schools was assembled.

A detailed review of this list led to125 schools with very high concentrations of low-income students and a certain reputation for academic excellence.

From this secondary list, 21 schools were chosen to appear in this book. Not all of the schools originally selected wanted to participate. Still others were positively forbidden to be included. For others it was impossible to verify their achievement scores or the verification process itself revealed a record of achievement not worth reporting. In the end, the 21 schools included in this study were chosen because they represent a broad cross-section of American schools that provide an outstanding education to their students regardless of race, income level, or family background. Except where noted, all of the schools studied here have a building-wide average on national academic achievement tests at or above the 66th percentile, even though 75 percent or more of their students qualify for the free or reduced-price lunch.

The principals from this final list of 21 schools were then interviewed and asked to provide recent test score data; background information on the history, policies, and procedures of their school; and any other material that might explain the specific practices that account for the academic achievement of their students. Finally, site visits and personal interviews with the principals, teachers, students, and parents of children in these schools made up the last body of materials incorporated into this study.

Low-income is the term most often used throughout the course of this study to describe the parents of children who are poor. For the purposes of this report, children identified as low-income come from families ranging from below the poverty level to 185 percent of that threshold. Children from these families qualify for the National School Lunch Program.

A given family's poverty level is determined by the age of the householder and the number of related children under 18 years. The poverty threshold established by the U.S. Census Bureau in 1997 for a family of four people was $16,400. More than one in every five children, or 14.5 million, live in poverty.

Children from families with incomes at or below 130 percent of the poverty level (or $21,385 for a family of four) are eligible for free meals at school. Because of their high concentrations of low-income children, many schools in this study provide both free breakfast and free lunch for their students. Children of families between 130 percent and 185 percent of the poverty level (up to $30,433 for a family of four) are eligible for reduced-price meals.

Percent Low-income reflects the number of children in a school who qualify for either the free or reduced lunch through the National School Lunch Program. For schools that do not participate in the program, this number is estimated by the schools based on the same criteria explained above.

Title I is a formula grant program that provides federal funds to state educational agencies and local school districts to support high-poverty schools.

Selected Bibliography

Adler, Mortimer J. *The Paideia Proposal*. New York: Macmillan Publishing Co., 1982.

American Federation of Teachers. *Raising Student Achievement: A Resource Guide for Redesigning Low-Performing Schools*. Washington, DC: American Federation of Teachers, 1997.

American Institutes for Research. *An Educators' Guide to Schoolwide Reform*. Arlington: Educational Research Service, 1999.

Bennett, William J. *Schools That Work: Educating Disadvantaged Children*. Washington, DC: Department of Education, 1987.

Berman, Paul and Cheryl Fields. *High Performance Learning Communities*. Emeryville: RPP International, Inc., 1998.

Bilskie, Amy L. *Lessons Learned from Successful Public Schools*. Atlanta: Public Policy Foundation, 1997.

Burtless, Gary, ed. *Does Money Matter?* Washington, DC: The Brookings Institution, 1996.

Chubb, John E. and Terry M. Moe. *Politics, Markets, and America's Schools*. Washington, DC: The Brookings Institution, 1990.

Connell, Noreen. *Beating the Odds: High-Achieving Elementary Schools in High-Poverty Neighborhoods*. New York: Education Priorities Panel, 1999.

Coulson, Andrew J. *Market Education: The Unknown History*. New Brunswick:Transaction Press, 1999.

Cushmann, Kathleen. "How School Can Work Better for the Kids Who Need the Most." *Challenge Journal*. Providence: The Annenberg Challenge, Spring 1999.

Duncan, Greg and Jeanne Brooks-Gunn, eds. *Consequences of Growing Up Poor*. New York: Russell Sage Foundation, 1997.

Fashola, Olatokunbo S. and Robert E. Slavin. "Schoolwide Reform Models: What Works?" *Phi Delta Kappan*. January 1998.

Hanushek, Erik A. *Making Schools Work: Improving Performance and Controlling Costs*. Washington, DC: The Brookings Institution, 1994.

Haycock, Kati. *Dispelling the Myth: High Poverty Schools Exceeding Expectations*. Washington, DC: The Education Trust, 1999.

Hirsch, E.D., Jr. *The Schools We Need and Why We Don't Have Them*. New York: Doubleday, 1996.

Johnson, Joe, *et al. Successful Texas Schoolwide Programs: Research Study Results*. Austin: STAR Center, 1997.

Mathews, Jay. *Escalante*. New York: Henry Holt and Company, 1988.

Mayer, Susan E. *What Money Can't Buy*. Cambridge: Harvard University Press, 1997.

Monroe, Lorraine. *Nothing's Impossible*. New York: Public Affairs, 1997.

Moss, Mike. *Interim Report on Texas Public Schools*. Austin: Texas Education Agency, 1997.

Myers, David E. *The Relationship between School Poverty Concentration and Students' Reading and Math Achievement and Learning.* Washington DC: National Institute of Education, 1986.

National Center for Education Statistics. *National Assessment of Educational Progress, NAEP 1996 Trends in Academic Progress.* Washington, DC: U.S. Department of Education, 1997.

New American Schools. *Blueprint for School Success.* Arlington: Educational Research Services, 1998.

New American Schools. *Working Towards Excellence: Examining the Effectiveness of New American Schools Designs,* 1998.

Ravitch, Diane and Joseph P. Viteritti, eds. *New Schools for a New Century.* New Haven: Yale University Press, 1997.

Ravitch, Diane. *Brookings Papers on Education Policy.* Washington, DC: The Brookings Institution, 1998.

Sanders, William L. and June C. Rivers. *Cumulative and Residual Effects of Teachers on Future Student Academic Achievement.* Knoxville: University of Tennessee, 1996.

Schlechty, Phillip C. *Inventing Better Schools.* San Francisco: Jossey-Bass Publishers, 1997.

Stringfield, Sam, *et al. Urban and Suburban/Rural Special Strategies for Educating Disadvantaged Children.* Washington, DC: U.S. Department of Education, 1997.

Stringfield, Sam, *et al.* eds. *Bold Plans for School Restructuring.* New Jersey: Lawrence Erlbaum Associates, 1996.

Suskind, Ron. *A Hope in the Unseen: An American Odyssey from the Inner City to the Ivy League.* New York: Broadway Books, 1998.

Toch, Thomas, *et al.* "Outstanding High Schools." *U.S News & World Report,* January 18,1999.

U.S. Congress. House Subcommittee on Oversight and Investigations. *Education at a Crossroads: What Works and What's Wasted in Education Today*, 1998.

U.S. Department of Education. *Turning Around Low-Performing Schools: A Guide for State and Local Leaders*. Washington, DC: U.S. Department of Education, 1998.

U.S. Department of Education. *What Works: Research About Teaching and Learning*. Washington, DC: U.S. Department of Education, 1996.

Walk, Ron. "Strategies for Fixing Failing Public Schools." *Education Week*, November 4, 1998.

Zill, Nicholas. *Poverty and Educational Achievement: An Analysis Plan*. Washington, DC: National Institute of Education, 1985.

About the Author

Samuel Casey Carter is a Bradley Fellow at the Heritage Foundation, a public policy research institute in Washington, D.C. Carter is the former executive editor of *Crisis*, the monthly journal of religion, culture, and public policy founded by Michael Novak.

After receiving his B.A. in Philosophy and Mathematics at St. John's College in Annapolis, Carter studied for his licentiate in theology at Blackfriars, Oxford. He is now finishing his doctoral dissertation on the Phenomenology of Jacob Klein for the School of Philosophy at the Catholic University of America.